D.A.U.G.H.T.E.R.S.

D.A.U.G.H.T.E.R.S.

Discovering Your Identity
from Your Heavenly Father

Chanel Moore

Heavenly
Light Press
Alpharetta, GA

ISBN: 978-1-63183-895-8 - Paperback
eISBN: 978-1-63183-896-5 - ePub
eISBN: 978-1-63183-897-2 - mobi

Printed in the United States of America   0 8 1 8 2 0

☺ This paper meets the requirements of ANSI/NISO Z39.48-1992 (Permanence of Paper)

This book is dedicated to daughters everywhere.
May you find the hope and encouragement you prayed for, and
the comfort and purpose that only a loving Heavenly Father
can provide. He's waiting with arms open wide.

Contents

Introduction: What Does It Mean?

So you have not received a spirit that makes you fearful slaves. Instead, you received God's Spirit when he adopted you as his own children. Now we call him, "Abba, Father."

—Romans 8:15 (NLT)

What does it mean to be a daughter? That was the question. And although I had come up with this acronym—D.A.U.G.H.T.E.R.S.—that was great, that was inspiring and encouraging, I'd never really asked myself what it meant to be a daughter.

What did it mean? What did it mean to not just be any daughter, but to be the daughter of a King?

That's when I realized that maybe I didn't fully know—that maybe I hadn't sat down and thought about what it really meant to belong. Because isn't that part of being a daughter? Having a sense of belonging to someone, to some family? Yet, here I was, claiming to belong to a special family without a full understanding of my role as a daughter in it.

We live in a world where the impression of a father figure stirs up pain instead of persistence. Where the lack of a present father has left women damaged instead of dynamic as they search for that sense of belonging throughout life. Unfortunately, understanding that we have a loving Heavenly Father has lost its appeal due to the lack of zeal in our earthly ones.

Not only that, but we live in a world where mothers

find it hard to encourage their daughters and prepare them for the struggles ahead. Due to the growing demands of life, we force ourselves to grow into women as soon as possible and shed the skin of girlhood. Therefore, as endearing as the term "daughter" was meant to be, it is instead replaced with the idea of childlikeness rather than maturity. And for many of us, that's a problem.

However old you are, you are a daughter. God is King and a loving Heavenly Father. And as His daughter, you are a princess. And if the term "daughter" casts images of a child in your head, it's okay, because God loves children. And God loves you.

First and foremost, you need to know this: You matter. You're not kind of a big deal; you *are* a big deal. And it is my hope that by the end of this book you will be able to come to grips with just how much you matter. Although there is still so much to share and learn on the journey to self-discovery for your identity as a daughter, the focus will be on the acronym D.A.U.G.H.T.E.R.S. As you read, I hope and pray that you will personally learn even more what the term "daughter" means to you.

Daughters are dynamic, authentic, unique, gracious, hopeful, triumphant, empowered, resilient, and successful. While these descriptions are personality traits, they also represent who or what we can be in situations or circumstances. Each word chosen represents a powerful personality trait not to be taken lightly. With each trait described, we will look at a woman from the Bible who I believe displayed this type of character.

I can put words on the pages, but it will ultimately be up to you to discover what being a daughter means in your life at this particular time. As a daughter, you have influence. As a daughter, you belong to an Almighty King.

And as His daughter, you have the right to display that powerful influence for your Father's glory.

So, what does it mean to be a daughter? Let's find out.

Lord God, watch over and protect this reader. You know the plans and purposes You have for her life. May the words that she reads be relevant to her. May she see how much You love her and have always loved her. In Jesus's name, amen.

Chapter 1

Dynamic

Wise choices will watch over you. Understanding will keep you safe. Wisdom will save you from evil people, from those whose words are twisted.
—Proverbs 2:11–12 (NLT)

Have you ever seen what dynamite can do? Well, in short, an entire building can be reduced to rock and rubble with enough dynamite. Dynamite has the ability to completely change the scene of what was once a sturdy building built on an even sturdier foundation.

When I hear the word "dynamic," I can't help but associate it to the word "dynamite." As a daughter, whether you believe it or not, whether you know it or not, you are dynamic. In a sense, you are dynamite.

The definition of "dynamic" is a force that stimulates change or progress within a system or process. As a dynamic daughter, it's possible for you to stimulate change or progress. We are agents of change. We are dynamic. And we have the ability to stimulate change or progress within our schools, our jobs, our church, and our community. Do you think this is possible? If not, let me encourage you, it is. In fact, it has been done before.

Have you ever heard of Esther? She is in the Bible. She is Queen Esther, to be correct. But before you use the fact that she was a queen to make an assumption, just know that that wasn't always her path. Esther had a very humble beginning. She wasn't born into royalty, and don't forget that being a woman during "Bible times" wasn't exactly considered grounds for moving up in the societal hierarchy. In fact, women having rights to speak amongst men was likely frowned upon. However, Esther, with odds stacked against her, was dynamic, and we'll see why.

I must admit, the life of Esther is one of my favorite historical accounts. I will give a brief synopsis so that you can get the gist, but trust me, reading it for yourself is much better.

ESTHER'S STORY

So, Esther was a young girl who was adopted by her cousin after her parents passed. Later, the king was in search of a replacement queen after banishing his former. More or less, he had a beauty contest and brought in beautiful virgins throughout the land. Esther, being both, was chosen to be queen.

During this time, there was a plot by a man named Haman to kill her people, the Jews. Esther, obeying her cousin, had kept her identity a secret all that time. However, as this evil plan came closer to fruition, she revealed it to the king. In an interesting turn of events, the person seeking the destruction of all Jews was thus killed, and Esther had the opportunity to speak with the king about saving the Jews from the decree he passed against her people.

Again, trust me, it is way more interesting than what I just shared. What's interesting is a well-known line that Esther shares with her cousin about helping the Jews. After challenging Esther to take a risk for her people, her cousin, Mordecai, says, "If you keep quiet at a time like this, deliverance and relief for the Jews will arise from some other place, but you and your relatives will die. Who knows if perhaps you were made queen for just such a time as this?" To which Esther replies, "If I must die, I must die" (Esther 4:14–16, NLT), because to go to the king without him asking for your presence was a life-or-death matter.

Now, based on our definition of "dynamic," I think it's safe to say Esther fits the description. Because of Esther's courage to speak up and take a risk, she was able to save her nation. Talk about stimulating change!

What if? Maybe that should be the question you're asking yourself today. What if you don't? What if you do? Simply ask yourself, "What if?"

Can I be honest? I have to ask myself that question often. What if I don't write this book? What if God chooses someone else to complete this project? Isn't that a scary thought? For me, it is. The thought of God using someone else for a task He called me to makes me cringe. So, sometimes I think maybe some of these women in the Bible felt the same way. Maybe they couldn't bear the thought of someone completing their God-given tasks.

What if Esther decided not to speak up? Or, what if Esther thought her beauty was all there was to her life? She could have been responsible for seeing a nation suffer, her own family included.

So, the question for us is, what are we settling to be instead of becoming what we were *created to be*? You're more than a pretty face and more than just a body; you're a walking agent of change. So, what do you see that you want to change for the better? Do *you* need to change for the better first?

Of course, you can see why Esther was dynamic, but let's

pinpoint a few things you can gather from the Bible story when you read it. These are the same things we must obey and understand if we, too, want to be agents of change.

TRAITS OF AGENTS OF CHANGE

Wise Leadership

What is wisdom? The most notable definition for me is one my grandmother told me when I was young: "Knowledge is what you know. Wisdom is how you use that knowledge."

So, how do you use your knowledge? How do you assess situations? Do you assess situations or just go into them blind?

To take my grandmother's definition further, wisdom, for me, has been preparation. How do you prepare for life? How do you prepare to use the knowledge you've been allowed to obtain? What will be the outcome of all of your preparation?

Also, wisdom has been discerning what wise leadership looks like and discerning truth. Knowledge is good, but a lot of knowledge with no godly discernment is really just ignorance. I'm all for learning; I teach. But, I also know that having a bunch of knowledge without godly discernment put into practice isn't very wise. As the Bible commands, we should get wisdom and develop good judgment (Proverbs 4:5).

The Pharisees had knowledge of a coming Savior, but no wisdom or love for God to discern the Savior had come.

So, what is wise leadership? How do you recognize it? For one thing, when put into practice, it aligns with God's will. Secondly, its guidance is for the benefit of others and not just one's self. Take Esther's cousin, Mordecai, for example.

Esther's cousin, Mordecai, thought it wise to hide her identity. It proved to be true, because at the perfect time she revealed her identity to the king to plead her case for the Jews. Adoring her, his concern for her people came from his concern for her. Esther obeyed wise leadership, even when she left her home.

Understand all leadership isn't wise, and wise people may not always be in leadership positions, but you can still benefit! Wise leadership could look like anything. It could be a parent, teacher, pastor, or boss. Just know that as you benefit from their wisdom, it is important for you to pass on that wisdom and hopefully become a wise leader, as well.

Timing

Remember how I mentioned that wise leadership should be in alignment with God's will? This includes God's timing, as well. We're in a hurry; God isn't. God knows the development we need. We're butterflies. Like butterflies, try to help us out of our cocoons before it's time, and you weaken us. Our wings don't grow strong, and we are reduced to life as caterpillars when all along we were meant to spread our beautiful wings to fly.

> Just because God doesn't operate in our time, doesn't mean that He doesn't know how to perfect it.

Now, could God create such a fascinating process for an insect and not have something better for His children? If the process for a caterpillar becoming a butterfly could be that intricately detailed, why do we rush our own development?

Don't rush out of your cocoon if God hasn't finished developing your wings. The beauty in development is that you are under His wings while He's developing yours.

How does timing fit into Esther's story? Her story is practically all about timing. If Ether revealed her nationality sooner, it wouldn't have been as easy to tell the king about Haman's plan to kill the Jewish people. Haman's hate was so deep that he would have probably done his best to work out a plan to commit genocide against the Jews while sparing the queen's life.

Secondly, Esther plans a banquet to talk to the king. She doesn't reveal her reasoning, but instead asks the king to join her the next night for dinner again. The following night becomes the same night she reveals Haman's plans. Haman is later hanged on the gallows he intended for Mordecai (Esther's Jewish cousin that foiled an assassination plot on the king). Timing didn't work in Haman's favor, but God used it in Esther's.

So, how about you? Have you genuinely sought God's timing, or have you been rushing through life? Time tends to be refinement. When we rush it, we skimp on our own refinement. Or, we rush and miss God's divine providence.

I know it's hard to be patient. You want the job now. You want the house now. You want school to be over with now. You want to be grown now. But, don't rush it. You're being refined right now.

Due to Mordecai's wisdom and Esther's, she realized that the timing of her being queen was God-ordained. She also had patience that was necessary to reveal the wicked plot against her people. If timing wasn't important, she may have revealed her identity too soon, taken her position for granted, and moved too quickly in exposing the evil plot against her people.

Although we desire to speed up processes, they must be done in God's timing. Don't rush the process, because the process is the glory. We want to hurry and get to the next stage, but it's being in your current state that will make being in the next stage so meaningful.

Never forget, just because God doesn't operate in our time, doesn't mean that He doesn't know how to perfect it.

Selflessness

Selflessness is always an interesting concept. It's easy to both oversimplify and overcomplicate the concept of selflessness. Selflessness doesn't just happen because you decide to care less about yourself. "I get it—I care more about others than me right now and forever" aren't magic words that make selflessness complete.

At the same time, it's not so hard to put yourself on the back burner every now and then. I know, it sounds conflicting, but hear me out.

There is nothing wrong with caring about yourself. There is something wrong with *only* caring about yourself. It's natural to want to make sure you're okay, especially if you want to help others. In the event of a plane crash, they tell you to put your mask on first and *then* try to help the person beside you. Why? Because if you're not prepared, you can't help someone else get ready.

So, wherein lies the problem? The problem with selfishness is that people tend to only think about how they will be affected. The problem is when we choose to ignore the well-being of others because our needs are being met.

Look at Esther. Initially, she probably did think the decree didn't affect her. After all, Esther was the beloved queen. It took a heart-check from Mordecai for her to realize, "Hey, this does affect me and millions of lives. I've got to do something!" Because she put herself aside, she was able to save millions of lives.

I wonder how God would use us if we didn't only focus on ourselves. I wonder how God would change the world when self-centered people become others-centered people. I truly wonder what all God wants to do for people who are for people. I wonder. Do you? Can He start with you and me?

Esther eventually understood the need to be selfless. The lives of others became more important than her own, so much so that she was willing to sacrifice it for them. As the adage goes, "Selflessness isn't thinking less of yourself, but thinking of yourself less." You can't want to change the world and focus only on yourself at the same time.

> What does God want to do for people who are for people?

IGNITE

One cannot truly be dynamic without wisdom, and one cannot be wise without understanding it is all God's timing. And we will never know how to be selfless if we are self-centered.

Esther shows us the change that is possible when we're willing to learn and sacrifice. Esther shows us that something dynamic takes place when daughters ignite. We see what happens when wisdom, timing, and selflessness come together to perform God's plans. In short, lives are changed. In reality, lives are saved.

So, for the change that you can create and the lives that you can save, dynamic daughter, dare I say, it's time to ignite.

I MUST DO SOMETHING
(AN ODE TO ESTHER)

The lives of my people are at risk
Even before I was queen, I knew I should do more
than just exist
But what can I do
My life may be at risk, too

The king, I can't just go in and see
I have to wait, he has to call me
Even then it's not just a simple fix
Not with Haman and his tricks

It's way too risky, I can't do this
But what if it's as Mordecai said
I'll miss my chance to save the Jews
Then someone else God would choose

I have to do something
But what
I'll figure it out
I just can't give up, I can't doubt

I know, I'll invite him and Haman to dinner
Haman will think he's a winner
I'll address the issue over food
Hopefully this will put my husband in a good mood

At just the right time
I'll convince him of Haman's crime
And we'll see how it goes
God only knows

I'm putting my life on the line
We'll see what happens after we dine
If I die, I die, but I must see the king
I must see that salvation for the Jews is what we bring

NEVER FORGET

You are dynamic.

Think on It

1. What's the wisest advice you have ever received? How receptive were you? Did you apply it?
2. Can you name an experience when you saw God's perfect timing at work? What was the result?
3. In what ways are you self-centered? How can you think of yourself less to become more selfless?

Scripture Application

This is why I remind you to fan into flames the spiritual gift God gave you when I laid my hands on you.

—2 Timothy 1:6 (NLT)

Chapter 2

Authentic

I am rare, and there is value in all rarity; therefore, I am valuable.

—Og Mandino

You will never hear anyone say they have an authentic copy of something. Why? Because either way, you still don't have the real deal.

To be authentic means to be genuine, real, not a fake or copy. You, daughter, are authentic. You are the real deal. And you are the only one. I think Dr. Seuss said it best: "Today you are You, that is truer than true. There is no one alive who is Youer than You!"

There is a fine line between real and fake in our society, unfortunately. Daily, we're bombarded with "truths" that are socially accepted but are spiritually no more than lies. We've been made to believe things are real that are, in fact, only copies.

Take reality TV, for example. It is aired nationwide, and we are supposed to believe that these lives are the "real lives" of real famous/infamous people. Somehow, we're supposed to believe that a few sprinkled-in real moments make for the reality of their lives.

> The authentic parts of who you are, are the most valuable parts of your person.

Yet, this is the culture we've bought in to.

Romans 12:2 (NIV) says, "Do not conform to the pattern of this world, but be transformed by the renewing of your mind . . ." I believe that conformity takes place when we begin to see authenticity branded as wrong. And unfortunately, we've created a generation of women who fear being themselves, especially as a daughter of God. Truth be told, the authentic parts of who you are are the most ridiculed, but the most valuable parts of your person.

What do I mean by that? Well, let's take Leah for example.

LEAH: GENESIS 29–30

To choose Leah to display a positive character trait is almost unheard of. However, I'm doing it. Why is it unlikely? Because Leah was known for being unloved, for being undesired, to say the least. Leah represents a stage or point in our lives that we all go through. Leah represents those times we've felt unloved or unpretty. She represents those moments when we feel like we've given it our all and still it's not enough—you know, when you fight for the relationship and it still ends. Or, maybe it's when you look for love and still can't find it, or those moments when you work and still don't gain. Or it could be the times you try and try to beautify yourself, and still go unnoticed.

Leah, to me, is the realest part of our person, because it is in her efforts—success or failure—that we really see ourselves. We really see the parts that we dislike, or rather, the parts we haven't understood how to like for their uniqueness or genuineness.

Leah was like us. She thought she was conditioned for competition, and that being able to bear children would make Jacob love her since her sister couldn't (Gen. 29:31, 32). She compared her ability to someone's inability and thought it merited love. And we do the same. The realest parts of us compare ourselves to others, and we hope that we win. We hope that what's left of our authenticity will filter out our flaws and will show in our abilities.

How could we not, right? If you read Leah's story, it says she was older and had pretty eyes, "but Rachel . . ." (Gen. 29:17). My guess is that that had been the story of Leah's life. "But Rachel . . ."

Daughter, there will always be a "but Rachel." However, that doesn't make you less of who God created you to be. The real parts of us are sometimes ugly. They are sometimes shameful. They are imperfect. They are real.

Leah was imperfect. Leah was not Rachel. Leah was Leah, and that's all she had to offer. Yet, Leah lived in a world that liked to compare. My guess is a world that liked to compare physical beauty to inner beauty, which isn't very different from today's world. But, my hope is that we wouldn't be so quick to compare physical beauty to inner beauty or real to fake.

"A woman who cuts her hair is about to change her life." Those are the words of Coco Chanel. We find too much identity in our appearance. So, when we change our appearance, we're ready to change. Unfortunately, we forget that God changes from inside out, not outside in. And that's the most important change.

Within is where it begins. That's where we see the real and authentic. It's in the real and authentic that we really see what's beautiful. At the end of the day, Leah wanted to be loved. That's real, beautiful, authentic desire. And there's nothing wrong with that.

KEEPING IT REAL

Our world unfortunately places a value on fantasy instead of reality. We're convinced that we have to wear makeup to hide real blemishes. We're forced to believe that our bodies need to look a certain way, because in "reality" they are too much or too less of something. We're taught and teach others that the realities of our emotions are signs of weaknesses instead of strengths.

In essence, we're made to believe that fantasy is real. And unfortunately, we do. Here's my advice to you and to myself: In a world where you can be anything, be God's. And that's the realest advice I can give you, daughter.

With the emphasis and chapter based on being real, I'm going to keep it real. Let's not pretend. Being real sounds easy, but it's not. I feel like it's especially difficult for women.

> In a world where you can be anything, be God's.

We constantly compare, and people constantly compare us. So, to be real would require us to drop the comparison game and actually admit that we have flaws—and for some of us, those are the very flaws we've tried so hard to cover up. We've tried to make sure we're good enough at so many things in order to eliminate or draw attention away from the flaws we hate.

Let's be honest: We all have flaws. And it's when we try to hide them or pretend that we don't that we stress ourselves out. I am very flawed. I make mistakes. When I lose my temper, when I face rejection, or when I struggle with the right words to write this book, I'm reminded of them. But the most rewarding moments I can think of in my life are when I have admitted these flaws and asked

God to do what only He can do with them. It's been in these humbling moments that God has used me most to encourage others and encourage myself in the fact that even with my imperfect pieces, He still creates a masterpiece. "For we are God's masterpiece. He has created us anew in Christ Jesus, so we can do the good things he planned for us long ago" (Ephesians 2:10, NLT).

> Even if we are flawed, we can at least be authentic.

And like Leah, the more we try to earn love, the more we try to cover up, the more rejected we may end up feeling. But the more we realize the real truth that God created us to be authentic, the more at peace we can become with ourselves.

The world will not change its opinion of us. It won't change its opinion of reality. But we can change ourselves. We can change how we view authenticity. Even if we are flawed, we can at least be authentic. So, how do we begin this process? Let's take a look at Leah to see how.

LESSONS FROM LEAH

Who Are You?

There will always be someone else, but who are you? Do you know? This isn't to burst your bubble or ruin your confidence or self-esteem. In fact, this is to help you. There will always be someone else. Face it, someone will always be prettier, smarter, funnier, etc. Truth be told, that doesn't even have to matter, because the question is, who are you?

In a world that wants you to compete, who do you

choose to compete with? Are you competing with the world of people out there, or the person you used to be? Can I recommend a choice? Choose to compete with yourself. Choose to be a little better than you once were.

When it's all said and done, God isn't going to ask you why you didn't become more like any person other than Jesus Christ. He's not going to ask you about your sister. He's not going to ask you about the competition. He's going to ask you about you. "So then each one of us will give an account of himself to God" (Romans 14:12, NASB).

How important do you think it is to have an answer when He asks? You are His. In a world full of chaos, comparisons, and confusion, do you know that? You are His.

Reality Is Beautiful

Fantasy is fun, but reality is forever.

Reality is beautiful. Reality is here and now. God created a real world for us to live in. And even though this world promotes fantasy, reality is what God planned.

Fantasy is fun, but reality is forever. Reality is eternal. God is eternal, so where do you choose to be? Hopefully, you choose eternity with Him.

Unfortunately, we often times choose anything other than reality. We have been convinced that what is real is not enough. If only we would understand that God created us to enjoy a relationship with Him in real life, and not in some fantasy world. Where would we be?

Living in the real world is okay. In fact, I'm sure you might agree that more people need to live in the real world. In real life, there are real problems. In real life, there are real flaws. In real life, there are really hard situations. In real life, we have real needs. And there it is—there is the beauty in real life.

In real life, there are real needs, which means there is a real need for God. Understand this: God created us with needs because He can meet them! In a fantasy world, there aren't needs. Therefore, there is no need for God in a fantasy world. In the real world, there is a real need for God and God only.

Enjoy real life. Enjoy needing God, because as your Father, He enjoys being needed and wanted by His daughter. Bask in the beauty that you have a Father that wants to be needed because He can provide.

God Values Authenticity

The world may not value authenticity, but God does. God always will. He created you to be you. So, God isn't pleased when we try to be or desire to be anyone or anything other than His creation. As Oscar Wilde has said, "Be yourself. Everyone else is already taken."

God isn't waiting to love you.

Ask yourself, if God wanted everyone to be the same, would He have created so many different people? If God wanted you to be like anyone else (other than Jesus Christ, of course), would He have made you the way you are? It's highly doubtful.

God values the real, authentic you, not who you hope to be or maybe even pretend to be. While we all should always strive to be a better version of ourselves through a relationship with Jesus Christ, isn't it reassuring to know that God still loves you as you are? Isn't it nice to know that God isn't waiting to love you?

THE REAL DEAL

Have you ever heard of the idiom "the real deal"? The textbook definition for this idiom is a person or thing that is superior or impressive and worthy of appreciation. That's what you are. You are the real deal.

Never let the world convince you that you are less than. Leah was loved by God, even if she wasn't loved by her husband. Although Leah may not have realized that, it doesn't change the fact that it was true. And even if those you sought to love don't love you in return, God does. God loves you.

We believe our real selves aren't worth loving. We believe we've made too many mistakes. We believe we aren't pretty enough. We believe that we are less than worthy of love, and we are even told that. But God does not say that.

God says that you are worth loving. God says that you've never made too many mistakes for Him to forgive them. God says that you are beautiful. God says that you are His. You matter so much to God that He even knows the number of hairs on your head (Matthew 10:29–31). Since that is true, should there ever be any doubt that God cares about us? Should we ever wonder if we are good enough for God's love? Should we ever be ashamed of being authentically us? No.

The real you is who God *really* loves.

DEAR LEAH

Leah, did you ever know
God said you were beautiful
Just plain ol' you
There's nothing you had to do

Your husband might not have cared
But you never needed to be scared
That love wouldn't reach you
Because God's love is so true

Leah, to God you were never dull
In fact, you were full
You would be surprised
At how much sparkle God put into your eyes

God says, The way that man sees, I never do
I've always valued you
I value your authenticity
Because that's who I created you to be

Leah, be a good listener
This was never a competition between you and your
sister
And although I will bless the nation you have birthed
You didn't need children to have worth

You are not the other sister
You're my beloved daughter
And to think any less of yourself
Means you don't know your own wealth

D.A.U.G.H.T.E.R.S.

Leah, you never had to settle for the title "unloved"
Because the God above
Never hoped for Rachel, but got you
To Him, you were never see-through

NEVER FORGET

You are you because that's who God created you to be, and that's who God chooses to love.

Think on It

1. How would you describe yourself? Why?
2. In what ways have you chosen fantasy over reality? Music, movies, beauty, appearance?
3. How does it feel to know God values you just as you are, blemishes and all?

Scripture Application

You made all the delicate, inner parts of my body and knit me together in my mother's womb. Thank you for making me so wonderfully complex! Your workmanship is marvelous—how well I know it.

—Psalm 139:13–14 (NLT)

Chapter 3

Unique

You are the only you God made . . . God made you and broke the mold.

—Max Lucado

Some people, some situations, some things are just unique. Sometimes there isn't any other way to describe it but unique. It's different. It's like no other. It's in a league of its own. It's one of a kind, unlike anything else. It's . . . unique.

Now, everywhere that you just saw the word "it's," I want you to put "I'm," because that's how God sees you and how He wants you to see yourself. You are different. You are like no other. You are in a league of your own. You are one of a kind, unlike anything else. You are unique. And to help you remember it, I will spell it "younique," because you are unique.

How can I be so sure? I've read that genes are composed of DNA, which is predicted to have over three billion base pairs in the human genome. We have approximately ten trillion cells, so if we lined up all the DNA found in every cell of a human body, it would stretch from the earth to the sun one hundred times. Do you know how far the earth is from the sun? It's over ninety million miles. Do

> You may be made of small matter, but you are no small matter.

you honestly think there is anyone else on this earth that can have the exact same DNA makeup as you? Not a chance.

Do you see how much effort God put into making sure that you knew how rare you are? He compiled one hundred trillion cells (that we know of) in your one body and made them a distance of ninety million miles times one hundred—all in order for you to know how rare and intricately detailed you are.

You may be made of small matter, but you are no small matter, that's for sure.

That's why it's important that we look at Mary in this chapter: a simple girl who becomes the Mother of Jesus Christ, the Savior of the world. Maybe she knew she mattered. Maybe she always hoped she might matter one day. Let's take a close look to see what made this simple girl so unique.

MARY, THE SIMPLE SERVANT

We must realize Mary wasn't always the Mother of Jesus. Mary was a regular girl. She was set to have a very regular arranged marriage to Joseph, and she planned on living a very regular married life, like most people.

Although Mary probably had regular plans, God's plans were unique for her. And because His plans for us are unique, they make us unique. God has special plans for us all that align with His purposes for us all. The Lord had this to say to the Israelites that were captives in the land of Babylon: "For I know the plans I have for you. They are plans for good and not for disaster, to give you a future and a hope" (Jeremiah 29:11, NLT). If God had plans for captives in exile, don't you think He has plans for you?

So, one day an angel appeared to regular old Mary and told her a very unique situation was about to take place—so unique that it could and would only need to happen once. And it was happening through her.

Mary had been chosen to bear the Savior of our sins. Talk about mother of the year, right? It doesn't get more unique than that. Let's look at some of Mary's "simple" subtleties that contribute to her uniqueness.

MARY, THE UNIQUE SERVANT

Ready to Serve (Luke 1:38)

God uses people who are ready to serve. Most people find their purpose by serving. Mary was ready to serve. She pretty much said, "God, if it's me You want to use, then use me up. What can I do, Lord?" So, He used her.

> God uses people who are ready to serve Him.

We know serving is good. We appreciate people who serve. We love having waiters. We tell our troops, "Thank you for your service." We value the idea of service. However, we don't typically want to be the ones that provide it. Why? Why don't we want to serve? Here are a few possible reasons.

- **Reason 1: We don't feel like it.** It doesn't sound good, but that doesn't make it less true. Most of the time, we really just don't feel like serving. It's not even a pride thing; sometimes it's just a time thing. We work all day, or we're in school all day. We're living life all day and the last thing on our minds at the end of the day is how to meet the needs of another person. We know we could—we maybe even know we should—but we just don't feel like it.

- **Reason 2: We don't believe we have to.** I guess technically you don't have to serve. But along with that technicality lies the truth that you must not want to be like Jesus. "For even the Son of Man came not to be served but to serve others and to give his life as a ransom for many" (Matthew 20:28, NLT).

Let's take a look at one of the most well-known accounts of Jesus in the Book of John.

John 13:1-15 (NLT)

Before the Passover celebration, Jesus knew that his hour had come to leave this world and return to his Father. He had loved his disciples during his ministry on earth, and now he loved them to the very end. It was time for supper, and the devil had already prompted Judas, son of Simon Iscariot, to betray Jesus. Jesus knew that the Father had given him authority over everything and that he had come from God and would return to God. So he got up from the table, took off his robe, wrapped a towel around his waist, and poured water into a basin. Then he began to wash the disciples' feet, drying them with the towel he had around him.

When Jesus came to Simon Peter, Peter said to him, "Lord, are you going to wash my feet?"

Jesus replied, "You don't understand now what I am doing, but someday you will."

"No," Peter protested, "you will never ever wash my feet!"

Jesus replied, "Unless I wash you, you won't belong to me."

Simon Peter exclaimed, "Then wash my hands and head as well, Lord, not just my feet!"

Jesus replied, "A person who has bathed all over does not need to wash, except for the feet, to be entirely clean. And you disciples are clean, but not all of you." For Jesus knew who would betray him. That is what he meant when he said, "Not all of you are clean."

After washing their feet, he put on his robe again and sat down and asked, "Do you understand what I was doing? You call me 'Teacher' and 'Lord,' and you are right, because that's what I am. And since I, your Lord and Teacher, have washed your feet, you ought to wash each other's feet. I have given you an example to follow. Do as I have done to you."

Jesus washed feet. Can you believe that? We won't take out the trash. We won't volunteer. We won't share food or time. But our Savior washed feet, including the feet of Judas, His betrayer. Think about all the things we're unwilling to do, and the things that Jesus, our Savior, very willingly did.

Actually, if we want to be like Jesus, we are ready to serve. Mary was most like her son, the Savior, when she was ready to serve. We are most like Jesus when we are serving like Jesus.

Honestly, it's human nature. Our human nature

associates greatness with accomplishments, greatness with followers, greatness with stuff. Whoever has the most servants is the most accomplished, right?

But God proves that greatness is sacrifice, greatness is service, greatness is His example. So, unless you walk in His example, you will never walk in true greatness. The greatest never need to be told they're great; they just have a need to serve.

- **Reason 3: If we served once, we've done our part.** Let's revisit the passage from John as we look at this third point. Below are verses three through five.

> *Jesus knew that the Father had given him authority over everything and that he had come from God and would return to God. So he got up from the table, took off his robe, wrapped a towel around his waist, and poured water into a basin. Then he began to wash the disciples' feet, drying them with the towel he had around him.*

Did you see it? Read it again.

Jesus knew that the Father had given him authority over everything, and what does He do? He washes *and* dries the disciples' feet. It wasn't enough for Jesus to simply wash their feet; He went the extra mile and dried them, too!

Therefore, it's not enough for us to think of the one or two times we've served and assume we've done our part. I venture to say, our service has just gotten started at that point.

- **Reason 4: I'm not comfortable.** I get it. You have to be out of your comfort zone to serve. That's why it's important to know what you're passionate about and start there. I believe your heart for serving will eventually begin to pour out in other ways once you start. Interestingly enough, I also believe that volunteering to serve in different capacities will help you find what you may be passionate about, if you don't already know. We have to be willing to surrender the lives we're comfortable with for the ones God created us for.

I understand. I love being comfortable. And just today as I asked God what I hadn't surrendered to Him, He said, "Your comfort zone." It was a one-two punch, but I knew it was true. Number one, because He's God. Number two, because I didn't want to do it. If it was something I wanted to do, it would've been easy to surrender it.

> To think we're excelling in our comfort zone is to have a false sense of success.

Our comfort zones keep us comfortable. It's where we believe we succeed and excel. The only thing is that that's just not true. We're not excelling because we're not being challenged. To think we're excelling in our comfort zone is to have a false sense of success.

The bottom line is this: You may not be comfortable serving, but did Jesus really die for our comfort? He didn't come for us to be comfortable. He came for us to be catalysts.

Humility (Luke 1:48)

Mary was also humble. She says God noticed this lowly servant. She understood her place in society, and it wasn't a powerful or notable one. She was a regular girl. And because she knew that, she was both humbled and happy that God chose her. She knew how big the task was, so to be chosen by God to do it would have been overwhelming. It would have been easy to brag, yet she approached her calling with humility from what we can see.

Is there anything that can keep us as humble as serving? Really, is there anything as humbling as volunteering to clean someone else's mess? Is there anything like tutoring a student? Is there anything like volunteering at a retirement home or homeless shelter? Not just for you to see yourself as a servant, but to see others in need of your service.

Maybe I'm reading into this too much, but I don't think Mary views herself as a lowly servant girl in a negative way. No doubt there was pressure all around her, and probably even temptation to say, *excuse me, I'm carrying you people's Savior. Don't talk about me!*

Jesus didn't come for us to be comfortable, He came for us to be catalysts.

Yet, what the Bible focuses on is Mary's song of praise or even simple references such as "she stored these things in her heart" (Luke 2:19).

We don't read about a boisterous woman. We don't read about a "tell it like it is even though it's not necessary" type of woman. What we instead encounter is a simple servant girl with humble beginnings.

In fact, it is in Mary's story that we can be reminded of God's love for everyone. He didn't choose a wealthy woman. He chose a lowly servant girl. He didn't choose a princess or a queen or someone with political influence, He chose a servant who would be His servant.

God can use anyone. And it makes me smile to know that He uses servants and He uses those who are humble. And I hope it's a reality check for you. That yes, God can use you as well. And He wants to.

God knows your background. He knows your family history. He knows it all. But if you are willing, God would love to use it all for His glory. God would love to leave you in awe as He puts the lessons you've learned and experiences you've had into work in your present day and future. After all, God used a servant to carry a Savior.

Praise and Worship (Luke 1:46–47)

We tend to beg and plead when we should be spending time in praise and worship, like Mary did. Being pregnant is overwhelming in itself. Now imagine being pregnant with the world's Savior. Not only that, but being pregnant and being young, and being pregnant and convincing people you are, in fact, a virgin! Yet, Mary went into praise and worship.

How often do we praise and worship for our circumstance before we beg and plea to get out of them? Not very often, right? I know that's the case for me. I tend to ask God for a way out instead of a way through. What I have discovered is that when my focus is on pleasing God, the pain doesn't seem so unbearable. It reveals itself as purposeful when I'm focused on God.

For me, when my plan is no longer in place, when I'm

given a task I can't even begin to face, my default is to overthink. I overthink, overanalyze, and pretty much get myself in a frenzy over things that God could change in the blink of an eye.

For some crazy reason, my default is a bit of panic (and pretend it's not) and then a side of worry (but act like I'm not). This is wrong, and I'm sure I'm not the only one. So, can we make a promise? Can we focus on God instead of circumstances? Can we take a page from Mary, who chose to praise and worship instead of panic and worry?

Mary had the biggest news of all time. Let's think about this for a minute, because being pregnant back then wasn't so simple. And it was certainly not okay to be pregnant and not married. Sex is meant for marriage (1 Corinthians 6, Hebrews 13:4, 1 Corinthians 7).

I'd like to take a moment to say if you've had sex and aren't married, God is willing to forgive you for that sin. Confess your sin and repent (turn from it). If you're ready to surrender and change, He's ready to change you.

If I'm honest, with my default set the way it is (wrongly, might I add), I'd freak out about being pregnant. So, I call these points "Reasons to Freak Out When Your Default Is Wrong."

- **Reason 1: Pregnancy is a big deal.** The entire process of pregnancy can be a big, painful deal. Thinking of the pain alone could cause a person to freak out.

- **Reason 2: Pregnant and engaged.** Let's face it: Naturally, if you're pregnant, you've been with some man. So, think about Mary's fiancé, who knew he wasn't the father. How much trouble could that cause? In fact, Joseph was going to break off the engagement quietly when he found out she was pregnant (Matthew 1:19–25).

- **Reason 3: Conceived by the Spirit of God.** I'm sure the people not only allowed the rumors that Mary was sleeping around, but also probably considered it blasphemous that she would say God made her pregnant.

These were just three of the things that came to mind. Unfortunately, I'm sure we've thought, or even heard or said worse, about someone today who is pregnant and unmarried. (On the opposite end, we also shouldn't flaunt pregnancy outside of marriage as if it were God's will for us to be sexually active outside of marriage.)

The point is this: Despite all the things that could possibly cause fear or anxiety, Mary chose praise. Her initial response (Luke 1:34, NASB) was, "How can this be?" The next thing we see is her saying she is a servant of the Lord and to let it come true (Luke 1:38). And from verses 46–55, we have Mary's song of praise.

So, how different would our lives be if we learned, like Mary, to have a default of praise and worship? Shouldn't we reboot our systems to factory mode using our manuals (Bibles) so that we can get there?

"Well, an angel appeared to Mary. I'd praise and worship, too," you may be saying. Well, Jesus came through Mary, and we have the Word of God at our fingertips (phones) literally. Shouldn't we praise and worship? When

> Change your default from panic and worry to praise and worship.

we boil it all down, do we trust God enough to praise and worship Him, even if we're scared?

You are God's daughter. He's got you. We must never forget that the God who protected Esther, Leah, and the many other women and people we will discuss is the exact same God who protects you and me (James 1:17). Can we praise Him for consistency? Can we praise Him for protection? Can we praise Him for being . . . Him? Hallelujah!

SIMPLY UNIQUE

In the end, Mary was simply unique, much like you. I'm sure if we asked her what her plans were, they'd be something simple. We must never forget Mary was "just Mary" before she had Jesus. In society, she was just Mary. She was a simple servant girl. But . . .

In the grand scheme of things, she was so much more. Before Mary herself had been born, God had chosen her for His special purpose.

To the world, you may be just you. You may be just a student, or just a girl or woman. You may be just somebody. But to God, you are a unique somebody. And God has a special, unique purpose for your life and His glory. Whether you choose to believe it doesn't make it any less true. So, what are you going to do?

Are you going to be ready to serve when He reveals His purpose to you? Are you going to approach Him and it with humility and gratitude because He chose you? Are you going to praise and worship God no matter how hard the path gets? Are you ready? Because if you are, I guarantee He certainly is.

MARY, THE SERVANT

Mary, young sweet Mary
In whom God chose to carry
The greatest gift of all time
Salvation of mine

A simple servant girl
Ready to change the world
Full of humility
In order to please God, she let it be

And when she was told the plan
She didn't withstand
Instead she chose to worship Thee
She took notice of His mercy

Oh, Mary, you were so unique
And to think society thought you would pique
If you, a servant girl, could marry up
That would lessen your suffering cup

But little did they know
What God planned to bestow
On His willing servant
To defeat the serpent

A plan that would make no sense
A plan that was so intense
A plan biologically impossible
But with God, unstoppable

D.A.U.G.H.T.E.R.S.

A plan that seemed too good to be true
A plan that could make all mankind new
And it was you He chose to use
No, He wasn't confused

He chose you because
When it was time to do His will, you wouldn't pause
No, you wouldn't hesitate
In fact, you would appreciate

You would take on all the ridicule
To allow God's will to rule
In your life
Despite those who would call it strife

Instead
You said
May everything you've said about me come true
It was My will you wanted to do

The Mother of Jesus Christ
The very one who would be sacrificed
Mary, the simple servant
Whose devotion to God was fervent

NEVER FORGET

You are simply unique.

Think on It

1. How can you show God that you're ready to serve?
2. In what ways can you practice humility?
3. How can stepping out of your comfort zone be an act of faith in God?
4. What's one way to change your default mode from panic and worry to praise and worship?
5. You are simply unique. How can this truth motivate you to live out God's purpose for your life?

Scripture Application

For we are God's masterpiece. He has created us anew in Christ Jesus, so we can do the good things he planned for us long ago.

—Ephesians 2:10 (NLT)

Chapter 4

Gracious

Don't forget to show hospitality to strangers, for some who have done this have entertained angels without realizing it!

—Hebrews 13:2 (NLT)

Online, "gracious" is defined as courteous, kind, and pleasant. Some interchangeable words are merciful, forgiving, tenderhearted, sympathetic, etc. Do you know anyone by that definition?

In essence, this type of person is nice. They seem unbothered, even when they are. They are forgiving, even when it isn't their fault, even if it's toward a repeat offender. They are sympathetic to those who are hurting.

Honestly, the "forgiving" part is something I could use some work with. I am forgiving, but I also feel like I have trouble knowing where to draw the line. One thing I have to remember—and you may have to keep in mind, as well—is that it doesn't say graciousness is foolishness. You can forgive someone and not put yourself in a situation to be hurt by them. Graciousness is forgiveness, not foolishness.

In this chapter we will not consider just one woman, but two when we discuss graciousness. The two women are Hannah and Abigail. Who are they? Well, let's dive in and find out.

HANNAH: 1 SAMUEL 1 AND 2

Hannah was one of Elkanah's two wives. Hannah had not been able to bear children while Elkanah's other wife, Peninnah, had. Because Peninnah had, she would take it upon herself to make fun of Hannah. Yearly, these taunts would take place as the family traveled to worship and sacrifice at the temple.

Bearing children was very important in society. One could draw the conclusion that the more children, the better. However, despite her barrenness, Elkanah loved Hannah.

After one particular meal, Hannah decided to go pray. There, she cried out in deep anguish for the Lord to look upon her sorrow and give her a son that she could give back to Him.

Wow, is all I can say. What a special vow!

While there, the priest assumed she was drunk because she prayed but there was no sound. After telling him she wasn't, he blessed her.

The next morning her family went to worship, and when they returned home, Hannah became pregnant. She named him Samuel, meaning "asked of God" or "heard by God." She also kept her promise and dedicated him to the Lord, where he lived his life in the Tabernacle.

Okay, you're probably thinking, *What's that got to do with graciousness?* Well, a few things stand out to me about Hannah.

- **Standout 1:** You don't read about Hannah responding in kind to Peninnah's taunts. To be of gracious character doesn't mean you allow people to stomp on you; it just means you choose kindness, you choose pleasantries, even though you could react differently. You choose to trust that God sees it, and thus He doesn't need you to avenge yourself.

So what? Someone taunts your hair or any physical feature? What if they make fun of your name or your family? Do you respond in kind, or choose an act of grace? Can I remind you that God chooses grace when you offend Him?

- **Standout 2:** The other thing to point out is that Hannah could have reacted much differently to Eli the priest's assumption of her being drunk. Here's a man of God assuming that this woman pouring out her heart to God is drunk. Talk about insulting!

Hannah kindly responds to his accusation by calling him "lord," a sign of respect for his position, and responds to his assumption with respectful correction. The way I'd describe Hannah's gracious character is having a reason to react rudely, but choosing to show kindness and respect. Could anyone say that about you?

It's easy to get on the defensive end. We take offense at a lot of things. Sadly, I think a lot of times we want to be offended, and even sadder, I believe that often times people don't even mean to offend us. If you're looking for an offense,

> God chooses grace when you offend Him.

you will always find one. I once heard a pastor say, "Simply ask yourself, *what if that's not true*?" Of course, in Hannah's case, we can see these are well-intended offenses, but in our own lives, what if we applied that question? How would our perspective of not only people, but situations change?

We see an intentional offense and a mistake take place in Hannah's life. She seems to respond to each situation without being catty or rude. Can we do the same?

LESSONS FROM HANNAH

As we've looked at Hannah's character by viewing her response to offense, I think it's important to also note other life lessons we can learn from Hannah. Hannah was gracious, but her most important characteristic is that she was a woman of God. So, here are a few lessons we can learn from Hannah as we talk with God.

- **Lesson 1: Be willing to give God the thing you want most from Him.** God needs to be number-one. In fact, He better be. And you need to know that what you want from God is not more important than God. In the end, Hannah was willing to give God the one thing she most wanted to receive from Him.

Are you ready to surrender it all before you have it all?

- **Lesson 2: Let life remind you of God's faithfulness.** The name Samuel means "heard by God" or "asked of God." I believe this was unique, because every time Hannah thought of Samuel, she would be reminded of God's faithfulness in blessing her with a son. Later, we see that Hannah is blessed with even more children.

If you read throughout the Old Testament of the Bible, you will see where pillars were built as reminders of God's blessings. Hannah's pillar was Samuel, because his very name was a reminder of God's blessing. You practically couldn't say his name without declaring the presence of God.

What reminds you of God's faithfulness?

- **Lesson 3: Pray fervently.** Pray with all you've got. Has there ever been a time that you prayed fervently? Have you ever prayed so passionately that it seemed like with your last breath you were praying? Hannah was praying so intensely that Eli mistook her for being under the influence of alcohol (read 1 Samuel to find out more about Eli as a spiritual leader). She was under the influence all right—the influence of the Spirit. Hannah was praying so intensely that words weren't even coming out anymore.

Have you ever been under the influence of the Spirit in such a way that you couldn't even express your need for God to move with words? When the only way to express yourself was a poured-out heart and no words? As John Bunyan says, "In prayer it is better to have a heart without words than words without a heart." In other words, your words mean nothing if your heart is not surrendered to God, because that's what God looks at.

Don't forget that as a daughter, we have a father. And while I will say we should never treat God as a genie when we want something, we should never forget that He is a good father. Good fathers don't see their children in need and not provide or comfort them. So, how much more would God, our Heavenly Father, not only meet, but exceed any expectations we would have of a good father (Matthew 7:9–11)? God may not give you what you want, He may make you wait for what you need, but either way, He will provide it or comfort you in the time of need, as a good father does.

ABIGAIL'S STORY: 1 SAMUEL 25

There are foolish people in the world. There are smart people who do foolish things. There is no shortage of inconsiderate people in the world. Wouldn't you agree? Sometimes we do nice things for people with no expectations, don't we? So, when we make a request, it's not that we want a reward for being kind; we just want people to be kind back. Well, this was the case between David and Nabal.

In short, David's men kept Nabal's flock safe. As David and his men happened to be around during the time of a celebration, he asked if Nabal would provide his men with some food. Sounds reasonable, right?

Nabal not only said no, but pretty much said, "Why should I share with outlaws on the run?" (See 1 Samuel 18–25 for details between David and King Saul.) In response, David, God's new anointed king, began to prepare his men for war.

Enter Abigail

Word of Nabal's disrespect reached Abigail, and she acted quickly. Thankfully, Nabal's servants told Abigail about Nabal's behavior, and she prepared food for David and his men that were coming toward them.

When she saw David, she bowed before him and accepted the blame for her husband's foolishness. In her speech, she also said the Lord has kept David from taking vengeance in his own hands (v. 23–31). As Abigail continued her speech and apology to David, he thanked God for her good sense and for keeping him from carrying out vengeance with his own hands. While Abigail hoped David would remember her, he ended up marrying her after her husband's death.

In short, Nabal found out about Abigail's intervention. As a result, he had a stroke and later died (v. 36–38).

So, am I saying that if you're gracious, you'll marry a king one day? Well, not exactly, but it's not impossible. What I'm saying is that gracious character is noticeable, even though it's not braggadocious or trying to be noticed. It's giving, and it intervenes when necessary. Let's see how.

Noticeable

Well, how do you know it's noticeable? For one thing, we're reading a real account about Abigail, so I've at least noticed it before. But way more important than me, Nabal's servants had noticed it.

In verses 14–17, Abigail finds out what Nabal has done to anger David. The New Living Translation version says in verse 17, "You need to know this and figure out what to do . . ." I'm sure fear was a motivation for the servants to reach out, but we have to pay attention to the fact that they went to Abigail about the problem. If you hadn't seen someone act wisely or kindly or graciously, would you go to them about a current problem? Probably not.

My guess is that they'd seen Abigail handle several situations with grace, and they knew she would likely have a solution or at least try to resolve the matter. She would certainly have a better response than their master had to David's kindness. And as we see, it turns out she did. Her husband may have been foolish, but it seems to be understood that Abigail wasn't, which was good for Nabal and his servants.

Giving

Graciousness can be giving. Yes, we give grace, but we may also have to see how to give when we need a little grace.

Nabal and his servants were in need of grace, mercy, and forgiveness from David. It's a blessing that Abigail was able to hear what happened and assess what needed to be done. She acted quickly, but wisely, as well. Verse 18 (NLT) says, "Abigail wasted no time." Grace may be patient, but it's never inefficient when it comes to timing.

Essentially, all Abigail did was bring gifts of food and wine to David. Ironically, this was all he had ever asked for, anyway. Along with that, she brought her apologies for her husband's foolishness. It wasn't her fault, but in a sense, she gave her husband grace by taking the blame.

Due to Abigail's kindness, she saved a household and a king, David, from making an equally, if not more foolish mistake than Nabal. He would soon be king of Israel, and David really didn't need a blemish like slaughtering Nabal and his household as a part of his record.

Intervention

As stated before, thankfully Abigail's intervention kept David from making a big mistake. Sure, Abigail could have just asked David to spare her life. She could've asked him to spare everyone but Nabal, but she intervened on behalf of everyone.

Her grace and humility saw a need for selflessness, and she acted it out. She made the wise choice, and the result was receiving David's mercy for Nabal's household.

In a sense, what Abigail did was allow her gracious character to provide wisdom and protect legacies. Again, she kept her future leader and husband, David, from killing a household of people out of anger. Had he performed this act, what would have been said of the future king and his patience?

Right now, how can you intervene to save someone's future legacy? Of course, it must be a God-ordained intervention. If it is, how is He leading you? How is He leading you to protect your own legacy?

WHAT'S INTERESTING

What's interesting about Abigail's story is that all this took place without her husband knowing it. He had angered David, who was geared up for a fight because of it. Nabal's very life hung in the balance while he was partying and drinking. He was unaware that his wife was working to save his life and his servants' lives, all while he partied the night away.

Did Abigail know her plan would work? I don't know, but I know she had to try. She had to hope that David would see past her husband's foolishness and see her grace and humility. And what do you know? He must have, because he says, "The God of Israel [. . .] sent you to meet me today" (v. 32, NLT).

So, where can you show gracious character? Is there a situation that needs a noticeable person of grace? Is there a situation that needs a wise assessment to know the next step? Overall, do you need to intervene for someone somewhere? Does a situation simply need kindness and courtesy to turn it around? Lastly, do you think anyone has intervened for you? If so, is it fair or paying it forward to not do the same?

Now, I'm not saying we always intervene. I'm saying you have to have a relationship with God to know when to intervene. But, if He tells you to, you certainly need to. Abigail saved a lot of people by taking the risk. And because it was right and in God's timing, it was worth it.

You see, a recurring theme is that these women have been willing to see the bigger picture. Their humility, their sacrifices, their risks have all ended up with a desire to save others more than themselves. That has to be the same for you and me. Are we willing to put down pride for humility? Self-gratitude for grace? Curtness for courtesy? If not, then we may be as foolish as Nabal.

YOU ALWAYS MATTER

What I'd like to make sure we keep in mind is that we always matter. It's easy to overlook Hannah and Abigail's lives, but if you really take time to study them, to study their responses, you see how much we can learn from them. Hannah's son Samuel becomes one of the most pinnacle leaders in Israel's history and not only crowns Israel's first king, but also King David.

What we ask for matters. What we do matters. As you saw in Abigail's life, we have the ability to influence very influential people. What could be a very bad reaction by someone can be defused by a positive response.

It's important that we never minimize our influence. Will we always know how greatly we influenced someone? No. I'd be surprised if Hannah or Abigail—or any of the women we discuss—could say that they knew hundreds of years later we'd use their character examples. We will never know everyone we influence, but do know that you do influence someone. Based on the influence you want to have, that could be good or bad news. I hope it's the former.

GRACE

Have you ever heard
Such a beautiful word?
The word "grace"
It's like a heavenly embrace

What does it mean to us?
What exactly is gracious?
How could it be defined?
Well, start with the word "kind"

What's one more?
Perhaps courteous or
How about pleasant?
Being kind, being courteous right in the present

Do you know someone with grace?
One who lets kindness take anger's place?
Hannah and Abigail were gracious
Even in the midst of the obnoxious

They responded with kindness
Even when treated with less
But during these tests
They saw God's faithfulness

Could the same be said about you?
When it's hard and people are mean, what do you do?
Do you pray fervently
And trust God and let it be?

Is there any trace
Of your extending grace
In your life
Or do you give into strife?

Ask yourself these questions
Go on, have an intervention
And know this to be true
God's grace is greater than anything you can do

God's grace has forgiven
So that we can go on living
And share what His grace has done
That's all part of the fun

Now, think about what God's grace can do
For me, and for you
Who are we to not extend the same
In Jesus's mighty name?

It won't be easy all the time
It may cost you a little or it may not cost a dime
But when I think about what Jesus did for me
Who am I to withhold grace and not give it freely?

NEVER FORGET

When God leads you to intervene, He's ready to use you to change things.

Think on It

1. Can you think of a time you acted rashly and without grace? How did that work out?
2. Can you think of a time you chose to give grace? How did the person respond? How did the situation work out?
3. Why do you think God blessed Hannah with more children after she kept her promise with Samuel?
4. Why do you think David later marries Abigail?
5. Have you ever been willing to give God exactly what you've been asking Him for? Why do you think this is such a significant sign of sacrifice?

Scripture Application

So if you sinful people know how to give good gifts to your children, how much more will your heavenly Father give good gifts to those who ask him.

—Matthew 7:11 (NLT)

Chapter 5

Hopeful

Hope deferred makes the heart sick, but a dream fulfilled is a tree of life.

—Proverbs 13:12 (NLT)

We hope a lot without really hoping, don't we? Our well-known phrase is, "I hope so." Does that phrase actually convey the true meaning of hope? Not really. It's more of an automatic response than anything.

What's another? Oh, "You've got to have hope." We pretty much use this as a response to someone when we're out of things to say. Or, if you're like me, you may just use the one word "hopefully." Short and sweet.

If we truly want to know what hope is, it's a feeling of expectation and desire for a certain thing to happen. You're looking forward to something. Other nouns to relate are wishes, dreams, aspirations, and so forth. And hopefully your wishes, dreams, and aspirations are things you look forward to.

Honestly, I don't think we know what it means to hope or have hope. In our society, we spend much of our day in dread, hoping that what we don't want to do is canceled. You know who knew what it meant to hope (or at least it sure looks like she did)? Anna. And I think Anna can help us with learning how to hope.

ANNA, THE PROPHET

Luke 2:36–40 (NLT)

Anna, a prophet, was also there in the Temple. She was the daughter of Phanuel from the tribe of Asher, and she was very old. Her husband died when they had been married only seven years. Then she lived as a widow to the age of eighty-four. She never left the Temple but stayed there day and night, worshiping God with fasting and prayer. She came along just as Simeon was talking with Mary and Joseph, and she began praising God. She talked about the child to everyone who had been waiting expectantly for God to rescue Jerusalem.

When Jesus' parents had fulfilled all the requirements of the law of the Lord, they returned home to Nazareth in Galilee. There the child grew up healthy and strong. He was filled with wisdom, and God's favor was on him.

So, to summarize, Anna's husband died after seven years of marriage, and she lived as a widow to the age of eighty-four. She never left the temple and stayed worshiping God with fasting and prayer.

Yes, I'm like you. A part of me is saying, "Well, what can we get from that? It's in the Bible, so I'm sure it matters, but how can it help me? I'm not old. I'm not married or a prophet." While that may or may not be the case, remember we're looking at what it means to be hopeful. So, what are the traits we see in Anna that could be evidence of hope?

Consistency

Anna never left the temple. Talk about consistent. When I read that, what I first notice is the dedication to God. It's showing that Anna chose to be where the Presence of God was expected to be. Anna was consistent.

Hope is consistent. You can't truly be hopeful one second and then completely discouraged and on the brink of giving up the next. Hope doesn't change because of our circumstances. In fact, circumstances tend to change because of hope. Hope will last forever (1 Corinthians 13:13). So true hope, from God, is consistent.

A bad moment shouldn't change your hopes for the day if you have true hope. Are your hopes crushed with even a whisper of bad news? If so, it doesn't sound like the foundation of your hope is in God.

Expectant

Hope is expectant. Hope in God expects God to move in some way. Hope in God looks forward to His movement. Anna didn't leave the temple. I venture to believe there's a reason she was at the temple all the time. I think she chose to be there. I think maybe she was hoping God would come. Maybe she was expecting God at some point. If she was, her wishes were coming true. And if she wasn't, God still didn't disappoint.

God came in, carried by Mary and Joseph (Luke 2:25–33).

Hope looked forward to seeing God at work, but even better, saw God. What if Anna was inconsistent? What if this day was the day she wasn't at the temple? What if, after her husband died, Anna became hopeless? What if she had nothing to look forward to? Without a purpose, we slowly perish. Or, as Proverbs 29:18 (KJV) says, where there is no vision, the people perish.

Keep in mind, expectancy doesn't always *know* anything is going to happen; it *hopes* something will. It's risky, but it's worth it. Isn't it? Expectancy may not know exactly when something will happen; it's just excited about the idea of the possibility of something happening.

Think about the pregnant woman and her husband. What's the phrase we use? "We're expecting." Well, they don't know *exactly* when the baby will get here, but they're looking forward to the arrival. They're anticipating their child's appearance into the world at some point. The fact that they don't know the exact day doesn't make them any less expectant or anticipatory, does it?

A very meaningful habit is fasting. It says that Anna fasted and worshiped. Fasting isn't something you do if you're not expecting a movement from God. Fasting is about going without so that you show your sustenance is found in God. Luke references Anna's fasting and praying as he recounts Jesus's dedication at the temple. Had Anna been fasting and praying for this moment in particular? We don't know. What we do know is that when people wanted or hoped for God to move, they fasted. I'd say God appearing in flesh was the greatest movement for them all.

After Hope

Here are some of the benefits of hope. Hope can make you happy. Hope gives you something to look forward to. Hopefully, your hope is in God, so there should be plenty to look forward to in your life.

After seemingly looking forward to God's movement, Anna finds herself in the Presence of God. And what did she do? She began praising God. She talked about Jesus "to everyone who had been waiting expectantly for God to rescue Jerusalem" (Luke 2:38, NLT).

Do you know what makes hope special? It's the fact that the feelings you had before receiving what you hoped for are magnified when that hope is in God. Before anything happened, Anna already worshiped and fasted to God. After God appeared, Anna praised Him. Because she hoped in God, her emotions toward Him didn't change after He did something. When hope is fulfilled, joy is amplified.

Anna's hope was in God. Even if she never saw Jesus, she never had to be hopeless, because her hope was in God. We don't hope because we want God to do something. We don't hope because we get something good out of it. We hope because God is faithful. We hope because we can have faith that God can. We hope that He chooses to work in our presence, but we're at peace and joyful because we know He will work.

Maybe this is a more tangible explanation. Say you play on a team (basketball, preferably). You, of course, hope that your team wins the next game, right? Well, something happens and you're not able to make the game. You call later to find out how the game went. All along, you were hoping they'd win, and you find out they pulled off a victory. Again, you hoped they'd win even without you, right? Yes. Did you hope they'd win with you, too? Yes. Whether you could be there as a part of it or witness to it, you hoped they'd win.

On a much deeper level, that's what our hope in God should be like. We hope to get to see what He does. We hope to get to be an immediate part of what He's doing. But we still hope that no matter what, He works, whether we're present or not, whether it was what we hoped it would be or not.

HOPE-FILLED

It's not easy to go from hopeless to hopeful. It's certainly not if your perspective is focused on the wrong thing. As a daughter, your hope should always be rooted in your Heavenly Father. His faithfulness should always encourage your hopefulness.

If you don't believe me, for sure take God seriously. He has a lot to say about the importance of hope.

Romans 8:24–25 (NLT)

We were given this hope when we were saved.

(If we already have something, we don't need to hope for it. But if we look forward to something we don't yet have, we must wait patiently and confidently.)

Romans 15:13 (NLT)

I pray that God, the source of hope, will fill you completely with joy and peace because you trust in him. Then you will overflow with confident hope through the power of the Holy Spirit.

Hebrews 11:1 (NLT)

Faith shows the reality of what we hope for; it is the evidence of things we cannot see.

Psalm 39:7 (NLT)

And so, Lord, where do I put my hope? My only hope is in you.

Psalm 130:5 (NLT)

I am counting on the Lord; yes, I am counting on him. I have put my hope in his word.

Proverbs 10:28 (NLT)

The hopes of the godly result in happiness, but the expectations of the wicked come to nothing.

Hope isn't about what you want; it's about trusting God. It's about looking forward to whatever God has planned, whenever He plans to share it. To be hope-filled is to look forward to the fulfillment of God's plans.

Anna's husband died, and she had no children. By societal definition, she had plenty reason to be hopeless. Instead, she dedicated her life to consistent worship and fasting, all while living expectantly through the hope of God. How can we do the same despite our past or current outlook?

> To be hope-filled is to look forward to the fulfillment of God's plans.

In conclusion, I'd like to leave you with one more phrase: "Keep hope alive." Really, please keep hope alive, because hope deferred makes the heart sick (Proverbs 13:12, NIV). Could you imagine what having no hope might do?

DARE TO HOPE

Some say dare to dream
But I say dare to hope
Dare to get excited
Even though you may hear "nope"

Yet hope changes our outlook
It changes our view of things
Our glass isn't half empty
In fact it's a spring

The feeling of expectation
The feeling of desire
Just the thought
Could spark a fire

If "hope deferred makes the heart sick"
Then imagine what hope can do
It can change perspectives quick
It could even change you

Hope is tough
It doesn't give up
It perseveres
No matter what

When all else fails, hope remains
Hope holds on like a chain
Three things will last forever: faith, hope, and love
Faith, hope, and love in what is above

This hope isn't humanly possible
No, God is the cause
True hope is in God
Even when everything is at a pause

So will you
Will you dare to hope?
Even when you can't see it all
Even without the full scope?

Do you trust in God?
Are your hopes found in Him?
If this isn't the case
Your light may go dim

Do yourself a favor
Read God's letter
For in it you will find
That hope in Him makes life better

NEVER FORGET

Look forward to God's will. Have hope, even when it doesn't look hopeful.

Think on It

1. Was there a time you had hope in a situation and what you wanted didn't happen? How did you feel?
2. Think of a time that you hoped to see God at work. How did that hope impact how you went into the situation?
3. How can you be hopeful in everyday situations? What does this act of faith in God look like at work or school or amongst friends and family?
4. Why should we have hope in God?
5. Is there anything currently not going your way? How can you have hope anyway?

Scripture Application

Faith shows the reality of what we hope for; it is the evidence of things we cannot see.

—Hebrews 11:1 (NLT)

Chapter 6

Triumphant

Leaders instill in their people a hope for success and a belief in themselves. Positive leaders empower people to accomplish their goals.

—Unknown

During the time of Israel's disobedience to God, a woman became a prophet who judged Israel. That woman was Deborah. Having been under the oppression of King Jabin and his commander Sisera, Deborah calls for a man named Barak and gives him the following message:

Judges 4:6–7 (NLT)
One day she sent for Barak son of Abinoam, who lived in Kedesh in the land of Naphtali. She said to him, "This is what the Lord, the God of Israel, commands you: Call out 10,000 warriors from the tribes of Naphtali and Zebulun at Mount Tabor. And I will call out Sisera, commander of Jabin's army, along with his chariots and warriors, to the Kishon River. There I will give you victory over him."

Barak's reply? "I'll go, if you go."

To which Deborah responds, "Very well, but you will have no honor from this victory over Sisera, for the Lord's victory will be at the hands of a woman" (Judges 4:9, NLT).

In short, the battle begins, Sisera's warriors are killed, and Sisera flees. He meets his demise in the tent of Jael, a woman. After their victory, Deborah and Barak sing a song that details the events prior, during, and after the battle. The final verse of Chapter 5 ends with "So there was peace in the land for forty years" (Judges 3:11, NLT)

As we've seen much in history, women weren't viewed the same as men. I'm often surprised when reading the role of Deborah and the level of respect she was able to obtain as a prophet and judge. I'm sure she wasn't without challenges, but she was living during a time when life really was likely considered "a man's world." Yet, here she is as a leader.

She is called a prophetess, which is a female prophet that speaks by divine inspiration from God, and she was also a judge. I think this is important to note, because there are a lot of women in the Bible whose names aren't recorded, let alone their occupations.

In other words, what I'm saying is that Deborah was a big deal. She was respected. She was a courageous leader. Most importantly, she spoke what God said. God clearly values women. Why else would she have such a big role in Israel's history? And not just her, but any of the women we've read about so far.

This isn't about starting a women's movement. It's not about seeing women and men as equals. We're equally loved by God. We have equal opportunities to accept Jesus Christ, but let's not get this twisted; there are certain responsibilities for men and for women. After all, this scripture in verses 8 and 9 give me the impression that Deborah wasn't looking to lead an army. She only agreed to go after being asked to go.

However, it's important that we don't mistake this: Women do deserve respect. Women do need to be treated like we matter, because we do. And note, because we deserve respect doesn't mean that others don't deserve theirs. The bottom line is if we didn't matter, God wouldn't have made us. God doesn't make purposeless things. He can't.

> God doesn't make purposeless things.

I bet Deborah knew she mattered. Why else would she obediently become a prophet and judge, knowing the endless ridicule that could come with the position? Most people don't knowingly choose a role that people will oppose, unless they know it's bigger than them. And again, we have our overarching theme of this book. It's bigger than you!

Deborah was a big deal. She was a triumphant leader, but why? How do we know the difference between a leader and a good leader, or a good leader versus a godly one? For starters, I think it takes a few things like courage, leadership, and honesty.

COURAGE

So, yes, Deborah was a prophet and a judge. Those are well-respected positions, but that doesn't mean that she was always respected. Even today, you have to be courageous to be a prophet or a leader. In our day of social media, one mistake and the public chews you up and spits you out, and that's with women having rights. Can you imagine the opposition hundreds of years ago that Deborah might have faced?

On top of that, she agrees to go into battle with Barak for the Lord's victory. From the text, we don't receive any indication that Deborah originally had plans to go into battle, but we see she didn't back down, either. I'm not sure if Deborah went into battle as an adviser or warrior, but either way she likely put herself in harm's way much more than if she had stayed home.

That's cool, Chanel, but I'm not going into battle. I don't need that type of courage.

Oh, really? There's a daily battle. There's a battle in the spirit world at all times. There's the battle within between spirit and flesh, and there are battles that we face in regular everyday life.

For everything God has created, the devil has worked to create a counterfeit. His daily goal is to get you to substitute the authentic for the counterfeit. There's a battle for your purity. There's a battle for your purpose. There's a battle for your soul. Satan's tactic is to get you to choose what he presents over what God does.

And we just thought it was our boss that didn't like us. We thought our husband was just crazy. We thought she was just jealous. Nah, it was the enemy using people in the battle to disrupt our peace. He was using people to battle for our confidence. He was using them to steal, kill, and destroy us in the battle (John 10:10).

Now that you realize what it is, have courage.

Psalm 31:24 (NLT)
So be strong and courageous, all you who put your hope in the LORD!

John 16:33 (NLT)
I have told you all this so that you may have

peace in me. Here on earth you will have many
trials and sorrows. But take heart, because I have
overcome the world.

Have courage in God. Deborah wasn't courageous in her own abilities, but in God's. Her words were "this is what the Lord, the God of Israel, commands you" (Judges 4:6, NLT). If the Lord hadn't said it, I'm sure she wouldn't have done it—and for sure not done it courageously.

Like Deborah, we can walk out in courage that God will give us victory when we choose His will. God, in fact, has already won the victory for us.

LEADERSHIP

If anything is obvious, I'd say it's Deborah's role as a leader. In Judges 4:5, it says she would sit under a tree and the Israelites would go to her for judgment. Who's letting someone judge them that they don't view as a leader? Not most people. Most people want a leader that they can trust, perhaps someone they relate to or someone they have common ground with. Would you want someone to be a judge that didn't have any of these traits?

Leadership is a big deal. It's important, because God's institutions all have a leader. Husbands are heads of households. Jesus is the head of the church. Leaders are necessary, because without them most things wouldn't get done. But there's a difference between being a leader and being a good leader. What are the main differences to me?

- **Difference 1: Good leaders lead for God's glory.**
  I've lived a life being called a leader. People believed that I had some kind of leadership

quality, and though I didn't see it, they did. So, I did things that put me in leadership roles: class officer, basketball team, etc. But the thing about leading is that most of our leaders can't lead. They want to, but they don't know how. And of course, those that can lead usually don't.

> When your goal is to honor God, everything else falls into place.

I was being thrown into a leadership role without a clue of what it meant. And I didn't really want to be there, either. Why?

Leading is really hard work. For every five people you can actually pacify, there are at least twenty that hate your decision. All the people who don't know the difficulties of leadership are steadily pointing fingers about how wrong your judgment is as they fade into the background in their own lives.

But somehow, I began to understand I was being called a leader because real leaders don't please the people. Real leaders know that it's impossible to ever have everyone on your side (and sometimes anyone). Real leaders aren't the loudest and the first to be heard; they're the ones that give you an unexpected nudge in the right direction.

In essence, real leaders work to please God. Real, good leaders know that they honor God by respecting people. They know that they honor God by giving instead of taking. They know that they honor God by following Christ's example as a servant. Therefore, anything that would hurt or disrespect God's children, they don't want to do.

When your goal is to honor God, everything else falls into place. You're kinder to people. You love people. You respect people. Why? Because you want to honor God. Under the umbrella of honoring God, everything else makes more sense and is better because of it.

Opinions stop mattering so much and offenses hopefully stick a little less, all because your focus is on honoring God. It's on pleasing God. If anyone has a problem with that, they've got a problem with God. And that problem is out of your hands.

Exodus 16:6–8 (NLT) is one of my favorite passages. Take a look:

> So Moses and Aaron said to all the people of Israel, "By evening you will realize it was the Lord who brought you out of the land of Egypt. In the morning you will see the glory of the Lord, because he has heard your complaints, which are against him, not against us. What have we done that you should complain about us?" Then Moses added, "The Lord will give you meat to eat in the evening and bread to satisfy you in the morning, for he has heard all your complaints against him. What have we done? Yes, your complaints are against the Lord, not against us."

What they're saying is, "You have a problem with how we're leading? Talk to God, because we get our instructions from Him." Real, good leaders can say that. They can say, "You're mad at God, not me."

- **Difference 2: Good leaders inspire others.** Good leaders inspire others to act. They inspire others to be better, to make changes, to strive for more. When is the last time you heard someone say they want to be like someone who's aspiring for nothing? Never. If you have, you might want to consider reevaluating your inner circle. Why? Because we should have an inclination to want more—for ourselves and for others.

I watched a show once, and they said something that has resonated with me to this day: "Great politicians are meant to inspire, not just be better than the alternative."

That's what being a leader is supposed to be about. It's supposed to be about inspiring people, not pleasing everyone. It's supposed to be about going against the grain, because it will matter at some point. Being a great leader isn't about just being better than the other option; it's about being the best option as someone who is concerned for people.

When you're concerned for people, you want to see them do well. You want to inspire them to be their best, even if sometimes you feel like you're at your worst. Think about who you follow and what they represent. Following a bum doesn't inspire you to do anything, does it? Does following an unkind person inspire you to be kind? Does following a negative person inspire you to be positive?

Ask yourself, "What am I inspiring people toward? Am I the bum, the unkind person, the negative nuisance?" Until you change those things, it will be hard for you to be a leader, especially a good one.

- **Difference 3: Good leaders are willing to serve.**

Matthew 20:20–28 (NLT)

Then the mother of James and John, the sons of Zebedee, came to Jesus with her sons. She knelt respectfully to ask a favor. "What is your request?" he asked.

She replied, "In your Kingdom, please let my two sons sit in places of honor next to you, one on your right and the other on your left."

But Jesus answered by saying to them, "You don't know what you are asking! Are you able to drink from the bitter cup of suffering I am about to drink?" "Oh yes," they replied, "we are able!"

Jesus told them, "You will indeed drink from my bitter cup. But I have no right to say who will sit on my right or my left. My Father has prepared those places for the ones he has chosen."

When the ten other disciples heard what James and John had asked, they were indignant. But Jesus called them together and said, "You know that the rulers in this world lord it over their people, and officials flaunt their authority over those under them. But among you it will be different. Whoever wants to be a leader among you must be your servant, and whoever wants to be first among you must become your slave. For even the Son of Man came not to be served but to serve others and to give his life as a ransom for many."

You can't follow Jesus's lead if you aren't willing to serve. We are most like Jesus when we are serving. If Jesus—God in flesh—came to serve people, why wouldn't good leaders be willing to do the same? Why wouldn't we jump at the opportunity to serve?

I'd be willing to say, if you can't serve, you can't lead well. Why? Because serving creates humility. If a leader isn't humble, he or she won't be willing to admit mistakes or accept suggestions or corrections. Do you want to be led by someone who won't listen? Do you want to be someone who doesn't listen? Would you want to lead people who don't listen?

John C. Maxwell says, "Leadership is influence." Leaders set the example. Leaders set the tone. If leaders won't listen, why would their followers? If leaders won't serve, why would their followers?

Let me sum leadership up with this quote by Arnold H. Glasow: "A good leader takes a little more than his share of the blame, and a little less than his share of the credit."

> We are most like Jesus when we are serving.

Good leaders lead for God's glory, inspire others to act, and are willing to serve. Jesus always says it best: You want to be a leader, first be a servant.

HONESTY

As we look at Deborah's last trait, it's probably no surprise that we're focusing on honesty. Deborah was honest, which means she could be trusted. After all, you don't get to be God's prophet and not speak His truth. That's simply not how it works. Look at Judges 4:9 (NLT):

> *"Very well," she replied, "I will go with you. But you will receive no honor in this venture, for the LORD's victory over Sisera will be at the hands of a woman." So Deborah went with Barak to Kedesh.*

Deborah kept it real. She said, "Hey, I'll go, but I'm telling you now, you're not getting honor for this." It would've been really easy for Deborah to pad Barak's ego. She could've said she'd go and just left off the rest of her statement. Instead, she chose blunt honesty. Notice I didn't say disrespect, but honesty.

She was honest that victory would take place. She was honest that Israel would be triumphant, but the credit wasn't going to belong to Barak. It was first off God's victory, and the person He would use to bring victory was not going to be Barak, but a woman.

> The truth can seem ugly to us, but it's necessary.

Not to overstate this point, but would people really come to Deborah if she wasn't honest? Would she be considered a good judge if she was a liar? I doubt it.

Honesty is important, whether you consider yourself a leader or not. In a world where lying is so common, it's important to remember that as a daughter, we're uncommon. We're supposed to be different. So even if everyone lies, we have to be truthful, because truth is God-honoring, and we always want to be God-honoring. We want to please our Heavenly Father by sharing His truth whenever and wherever we can. The truth can seem ugly to us, but it's necessary.

BE TRIUMPHANT

Deborah was triumphant. She saw a window of opportunity and courageously looked through it. And when that window became a door, she boldly went through it. Why? Was it to go down in history as a phenomenal woman?

No. It was to bring honor to God. It was to save God's nation of people. It was to be used by God.

And you can want the same. You can take the opportunities God has given you to bring Him honor. You may not lead a nation, but you may write a book that stretches across the nation. You may not prophesy a victory, but you can encourage someone to be victorious over sin. You may not even have plans on joining the fight, but your influence may inspire someone who does.

Deborah was a leader. She listened to God as a prophetess and led according to His will. Why can't you? Being a leader doesn't always mean you're in front of a big group of people. We have to be intentional about not overcomplicating what leadership is.

You may lead a friend, or a class, or a mentee. Leadership doesn't look like one specific thing. Leadership is being in any place where you can have an influence on someone or something. And a good leader makes sure that her choices are God-honoring, because what's God-honoring is always what's best for everyone who's following.

Lastly, be honest. Just tell the truth. "The truth will set you free" (John 8:32, NLT). Jesus said that for a reason. Good leaders tell the truth. You want to be a good leader? You have to be trusted. How do you earn trust? Be honest. It's that simple.

Today, if you're going through anything and questioning the outcome, simply ask God. Victory is in God. Therefore, it will be in what He says to do. I'm not promising an *easy* victory. I'm just honestly saying victory is in God. Take heart. Lead by following God, and speak truth into the situation — God's truth. Be triumphant. Your Father is.

COURAGE

Courage to take a stand
No matter the plan
Courage to speak the truth
Deborah was proof

She had to be bold
Based on what we are told
A judge and prophet
Fear was her opposite

And when she was asked to ride
She stood for Israel on God's side
What can we learn from her?
What can we infer?

That being chosen isn't easy
But it's God we must go on pleasing
That being bold isn't a gender role
It's trusting God, allowing Him control

Do you trust Him?
Even when it looks grim?
Have you rested in His control?
Have you given Him your soul?

Deborah was a leader, we know this is true
Deborah led well, trusting in God's view
That's what good leaders do
That's how they get through

D.A.U.G.H.T.E.R.S.

Will you lead well?
Will yours be a story to tell?
The story of
How you allowed the God above

To use you
To make you new
To lead others for His glory
There is no better story

NEVER FORGET

Triumphant leaders make honoring God their priority.

Think on It

1. Is serving difficult for you? Why?
2. Do you believe that today's leaders possess any of these traits? Where do we ourselves fall short in these areas? What can we do to change that?
3. We are in a battle every day. How can we stay conscious of that and daily choose God's authentic purposes for us, instead of the enemy's counterfeit ones?
4. Why is it hard to be honest? What makes the truth seem less appealing to our society?
5. How can you begin leading in a way that makes God's honor your priority?

Scripture Application

But among you it will be different. Whoever wants to be a leader among you must be your servant, and whoever wants to be first among you must become your slave. For even the Son of Man came not to be served but to serve others and to give his life as a ransom for many.

—Matthew 20:26–28 (NLT)

Chapter 7

Empowered

Truth is powerful and it prevails.
—Sojourner Truth

When was the last time you felt empowered? When was the last time someone made you feel empowered? Honestly, when was the last time you felt that you had the power to do something or change something?

See, for me, when I think of empowerment, I think of having the power to put it in God's hands. Once it is given to God, He will give me the power I need to do with it whatever He wants me to. Empowerment isn't about your strength; it's about His strength at work in you.

As women, we don't do a good job of empowering each other. A lot of time we end up envying each other rather than empowering each other. There is no need for envy. We're all equally loved by God and special to Him.

In this chapter we'll discuss the Samaritan woman at the well and the woman with the issue of blood. One was so moved by Jesus that she left their meeting in boldness, and the other was bold enough to reach out to Jesus and leave empowered through His healing.

Two women face two different circumstances and come out on top. When Jesus speaks to you, when He touches you, when He forgives you, your circumstances don't feel like they have to change anymore, because you do. You receive power from Him to take on whatever it is. Let's see how these ladies did just that.

SAMARITAN WOMAN (JOHN 4)

There's a lot to unpack in these verses, so let's do that first. Jewish people didn't associate with Samaritans. So, the fact that Jesus was talking with a Samaritan was against basic Jewish etiquette 101.

Next, it's noon, the hottest part of the day. Women didn't go to wells during the hottest times, but went when it was coolest. It's likely she was there to avoid other people. God is so good. She went there to avoid people, and Jesus went there to see her!

> She went there to avoid people, and Jesus went there to see her!

Jesus is where you need Him to be, even when you don't realize where that is. Jesus Christ was at a well in Samaria at noon. What are the odds of that? The fact of the matter is that He was there because someone needed Him to be there. This woman probably didn't think the odds were in her favor anymore. The truth is that they didn't need to be, because God was in her favor.

In their discussion, Jesus offers her living water. They discuss worship, and Jesus reveals what He knows about her past and present life. And through this, He reveals Himself to her.

Obviously, after meeting the Messiah, this woman was empowered. So much so that she runs to the village to tell everyone else about Jesus. In turn, when the other people come see Him, they beg Him to stay, and they believe in Jesus as Savior of the world.

Isn't that amazing? God's math is amazing. One woman at one well with one Savior led to the salvation of many.

There's only one you. What will you plus your Savior equal to? If you've confessed Jesus as your Lord and Savior, and believe in your heart that God raised Him from the dead, you will be saved (Romans 10:9). Take that first step. It's the best step. If you've done that and have received the Holy Spirit, then you've received power to do what God has called you to do.

It doesn't matter if the odds aren't in your favor as long as God is.

Acts 1:8 (NLT)

But you will receive power when the Holy Spirit comes upon you. And you will be my witnesses, telling people about me everywhere—in Jerusalem, throughout Judea, in Samaria, and to the ends of the earth.

Acts 2:38 (NLT)

Peter replied, "Each of you must repent of your sins and turn to God, and be baptized in the name of Jesus Christ for the forgiveness of your sins. Then you will receive the gift of the Holy Spirit."

So, what happens when you're empowered by Jesus? Life finally begins to truly happen. True purpose takes place. And as you begin to understand and walk in that purpose, keep the following ideas in mind.

Remember: When
Jesus Wants to Talk, Listen

Unlike us, when Jesus speaks, it's always because someone needs to hear it. The woman probably wasn't expecting a conversation at the well. But when Jesus asked for a drink, He was asking for a conversation, as well. (On a side note, I wonder if He ever got a drink. I hope so.)

How often does Jesus ask us for a drink and we leave Him thirsty? In your day to day, how often do you sit with Jesus and listen? He so wants to speak to you. He so wants to spend time with you. Don't you want to spend time with Him?

He knows how to encourage you. He knows exactly what you need today. Won't you allow Him to share it with you? Don't you want to listen? Don't you *need* to listen?

What would our lives look like if we listened to Jesus more? Seriously, if we intentionally chose time with Jesus over everything else, how different would we be? Try that today. Just tell yourself you're going to spend an intentional amount of time at His feet, just to listen to Him.

The Samaritan woman listened, and she was offered Living Water. Why would our offer be any different?

Remember: When Jesus
Offers You a Drink, Take It

Jesus was offering this woman a drink. He was offering her Living Water. He was offering her eternal life through Him. Today, He still does the same. Today, He still offers us Himself. And just like the choice was hers, we also have a choice. What do you choose?

This woman was so empowered by this offer that she went to tell others about it. You simply don't get a drink from Jesus and go about business as usual. You don't get a drink of Jesus and not want to share it with others.

When Jesus offers you a drink, take it. Always.

The beauty is that Jesus wasn't offering this woman some water; he was offering this woman some power—not her own power to change, not her own strength, but power and strength from Him.

Should any of us choose Jesus and choose to drink, we choose His power. Don't walk around thirsty when you don't have to be.

Remember: To Forget!

It looks like there are two things this woman forgot after her encounter with Jesus. And by forget, I don't mean that she actually had a memory lapse; I mean that those things just didn't matter.

1. **The water jug:** She left her water jar beside the well (v. 28). She left the exact thing she needed at the well—her water—and in her excitement forgot about it, ran back to the village, and told everyone who she had just met.

When you've been empowered by Jesus, when He's spoken into your life, you'll forget what your problem was. Sometimes you get to a place where it doesn't matter, because you're so excited about Him.

On this perhaps lonely, ordinary day, this thirsty woman left replenished. She came for water and met Living Water in Christ.

2. **The opinions:** The next thing she did was

something we all should do when we meet Jesus. She went and told everyone! She forgot about being an outcast and went straight into the village to tell people about Jesus.

Are you there? Do people's opinions matter to you more than God's? When you meet Jesus, you become bold enough to care less about what others have to say. When you meet Jesus, you want others to meet Him, no matter what. When you meet Jesus, you tend to forget about everything else, because nothing else matters except the fact that you met Jesus.

WOMAN WITH THE ISSUE OF BLOOD

If the woman at the well was empowered after meeting Jesus, the woman with the issue of blood was empowered by the *idea* of meeting Jesus.

Mark 5:27-28 (NLT)
She had heard about Jesus, so she came up behind him through the crowd and touched his robe. For she thought, "If I can just touch his robe, I will be healed."

I think it's safe to say that faith in Jesus can empower us based on this. Let's look closely at this.

Faith Stops Jesus

Mark 5:28-30 (NLT)
For she thought, "If I can just touch his robe, I

will be healed." Immediately the bleeding stopped, and she could feel in her body that she had been healed of her terrible condition. Jesus realized at once that healing power had gone out from him, so he turned around in the crowd and asked, "Who touched my robe?"

Matthew 9:22 (NLT)

Jesus turned around, and when he saw her he said, "Daughter, be encouraged! Your faith has made you well."

This woman's thought was that *if* she could just touch Jesus's robe, she would be healed.

Do you know that everyone has faith? We believe a chair won't break when we sit in it. We have faith our alarm clock will go off. We even say, "You gotta have faith." But for some reason, when things are really hard, faith is the first thing that wavers.

How much faith does it take to believe Jesus can change your situation? How much faith does it take to believe that you could touch Jesus and be healed? How much faith does it take to believe that if nothing else, maybe you could touch His clothes and be healed? I believe it would take all the faith you've got. And that faith empowered her to at least try.

Faith not only moves Jesus; it stops Him in His tracks, as well. Isn't it beautiful that Jesus responds to faith the way the situation needs Him to? Because of this woman's faith, Jesus stopped and turned around to respond to it.

Faith Heals

This woman had faith. I don't think we can deny it, but

I also believe that this teaches us that faith heals. Know that healing comes in many forms, not just in good health. Healing may be needed for broken relationships. Emotional or mental healing may be needed, or physical. Regardless of the type, Jesus heals.

My grandmother died from cancer, but I believe she is healed in Heaven. In this instance, healing ended this woman's condition of blood.

Why do I believe this is the case?

Luke 8:46 (NLT)
But Jesus said, "Someone deliberately touched me, for I felt healing power go out from me."

Jesus said someone deliberately touched Him, because He felt healing power go out of Him. Someone intentionally believed Jesus would heal, and he felt their belief pull healing power from Him.

Originally, I thought I was going to have more to say about this encounter, but I don't think I can say anything else without clouding the message here. Someone believed in Jesus, and He felt that! And because they believed, they walked away empowered by Jesus.

Praise break!

OUR STORIES

Why do our stories have to be any different? I get that we have different circumstances, but there's no reason we can't come out empowered just like these women. They had encounters with Jesus, and it changed their lives. Why don't you spend time with Jesus so that He can do the same for you? For them, it took a listening ear and great amount of faith. Does it take much more than that? Have we overcomplicated what it means to meet Jesus or to trust Him?

We have the best news and the most powerful news of all time: the message of Jesus Christ. And Jesus not only wants to empower us by telling us His message, but He also wants to empower us to tell His message *and* through telling what He has done. What are we waiting on?

Could you use some power today? Are you in need of confidence? Grab your Bible and a water bottle, and sit with Jesus and listen. Deliberately reach out to Him and see if He stops for you. I have faith that He will. His history shows that He always has.

FAITH WAS THE REQUIREMENT

They say Jesus heals
I want to see if He's real
I've been sick a long time
I've spent every dime

And penniless I sit
With my issue unfixed
I've heard about Jesus
But if He can't heal me, that truth will be grievous

I can't bear another failed attempt
I would almost rather exempt
Myself from the hope of being whole
But I cannot deny what I've been told

I refuse to continue to sit
Here as if I'm unfit
I refuse to continue bleeding
With nothing to believe in

So maybe I don't have to touch Him
Maybe just His clothes
I would settle for a sandal
Or better yet, a robe

If my faith would extend for just one reach
I won't hold on long, I'll just be brief
If I could reach out to Jesus for just one touch
I promise to His robe only briefly will I clutch

Here He comes
It's now or never
Call me crazy
But I know this touch will make me better

I've felt nothing like this
There's no feeling in this world
And if anyone says there is
Then their lies I will hurl

And after I touched Him
He stepped amongst the crowd
"Who touched my robe?"
He asked out loud.

There are many pressing against You
How could You feel the one?
And He said when faith connects to Me
I feel the work being done

And fearful I came before Him
And fell to my knees
"Jesus, I needed You
I had to touch You. Forgive me please"

And He looked at me and said,
"Your faith has made you well
Go in peace. Your suffering is over"
And right then I could've yelled

Jesus, thank You for noticing me on the way
Jesus, thank You for healing me today

D.A.U.G.H.T.E.R.S.

Jesus the Healer, and forever I'll know
Jesus who stopped for me while He was on the go

Jesus the Healer, and One and Only Son
Jesus, whose touch means healing is done
I found Jesus, who has healing in His garments
I found Jesus, and faith was the requirement

NEVER FORGET

Faith in Jesus is empowering.

Think on It

1. What do you think the woman at the well thought when Jesus spoke to her?
2. How do you think she felt after having a conversation with Him?
3. Have you ever placed your hope in Jesus? How did your situation change, or how did you change?
4. Why is it hard for us to spend time intentionally listening to Jesus? How can we better manage our daily lives so that this is not an issue?
5. Is there anything you're facing today that requires a big leap of faith? If your faith is in Jesus, why should you feel empowered to take it?

Scripture Application

And he said to her, "Daughter, your faith has made you well. Go in peace. Your suffering is over."

—Mark 5:34 (NLT)

Chapter 8

Resilient

God will use whatever he wants to display his glory. Heavens and stars. History and nations. People and problems. Be a doer, not a stewer.

—Max Lucado

As I sit and contemplate what the next piece to this book is, I am challenged. See, I want to tell you how wonderful you are. I want to tell you that because you're wonderful, everything will work out wonderfully in your favor. But I can't.

See, right now, I just left a job. I didn't love it, and neither do I love the current job I have. However, we needed to make ends meet, so work misery seemed to be the trade-off. And even though there is a sense of relief from my newfound freedom, I am still trying to find myself.

The ends still need to meet, and I still have to trust God with less finances coming in. But I need to be home. I am a little lost. I am confused. And I feel that I'm not in on God's plan. But He is faithful, and I will trust Him without knowing every piece to this puzzle.

So, why am I saying this? Because even though you are wonderful, circumstances are overwhelming at times.

Rather than write about all the things that have worked out in my favor, I have to write about the things that, quite frankly, I haven't understood. I doubt that you will be encouraged if all you read is a perfect story of my life. But if you've been discouraged by relationships, or job loss, or career confusion, or purpose pursuits, you will likely be encouraged by the truth that I've been there—and even now am in many ways still there.

As daughters, we are unique and authentic. We have unique problems and real times that are not ideal. To write this book and neglect to mention the difficulty of being a daughter would be a half-truth at best.

Yet, it is in the difficulty, and dark times, and the wavering that I have found it most meaningful to be a daughter. It's when I feel the most lost that I am reminded that I belong to a loving Heavenly Father. Without the trials, I miss the opportunity to run into the arms of the Father that is more than willing to listen and lead during the deaf and blind moments in my life.

To refuse to address the difficult moments in life, in essence, is to refuse to accept the need for a Father as a daughter.

Daughters are resilient. We spring back, we rebound, and we recover from adversity. And thankfully, we have a Father that cheers us on along the way.

RESILIENT RUTH: RUTH 1–4

Ruth was a Moabite woman. In essence, this means that she probably didn't have a background or family history of worshiping the One and Only God of Israel. She was married into the family of Elimelech, whose wife was Naomi.

Elimelech relocated his family to Moab. He later died and his sons married Moabite women—one being Ruth, the other being Orpah. Ten years later, both the sons died, and Naomi was left alone without her husband or sons. In the culture of that day, having no husband or sons meant you were left without a provider, and Naomi was in a foreign land away from family, on top of that.

So, Naomi's solution was to leave for Judah, her homeland, with Ruth and Orpah. Along the way, Naomi told the women they should return to their own mothers, especially since she had no sons for them to marry and nothing to offer them. Ruth, however, made a vow that she would not leave Naomi, and that Naomi's people would be her people and Naomi's God would be her God (Ruth 1:16). Thus, their journey continued.

Over the next three chapters, we see Ruth taking responsibility as a provider for both her and Naomi by gathering grain. It just so happened that the field Ruth gathered in belonged to Boaz, a relative of Naomi's husband.

As Boaz found out about Ruth's hard work and commitment to Naomi, he allowed her to have lunch with his harvesters and take extra grain home. Throughout Chapter 2, you can read more of his intentional kindness toward Ruth.

Upon hearing about Ruth's day, Naomi orchestrated a plan to get Boaz to marry Ruth. Out of faithfulness to Naomi, Ruth promised to do as she said. The plan worked. Boaz figured out a way to marry Ruth and become the provider for her and Naomi. Ruth, a non-Jew, married Boaz and found herself a part of the lineage of Jesus Christ.

Okay, what does any of that have to do with resilience? Well, let's take a look, shall we?

KEEP ON PUSHING: PERSEVERE

What happens when you lose something? When I lose something, I'm upset. What about when you lose someone? I'm sad when I lose a family member. Ruth didn't just lose something, she didn't lose just anyone; she lost her husband. She lost her provider. She essentially lost her livelihood.

In Ruth's time, men were the providers. You hoped to marry for love, but you expected to at least marry for provision. When Ruth's husband died, and Ruth's brother-in-law, as well, her hopes for provision died also. Remember, the men's father was already dead. With the death of these three men, three women had to figure out what life would be like for them. The overarching question would be, "How would they make it through?"

I don't know if you're married. I don't know if your father or mother is a provider. How would you feel if your sole provider died? What about if your second chance for provision died, as well? It would be hard, right? Today, we live in a society where women have opportunities to provide for themselves, and we can admit that it would still be hard to push through without our sole providers. Well, what if we lived during Ruth's time? I think we can agree it would be really hard.

Can I segue briefly? I love being married. I love my husband. We're very different—opposites in a lot of ways—but we love God and are committed to Him. Therefore, we love each other, and we're committed to our marriage. As a provider, my husband has always done whatever he can to make sure I'm taken care of spiritually, physically, mentally, emotionally, and financially. If he died right now, I don't know what I would do. In fact, I don't know *how* I would go on. I know that I'd have to trust God, but it would be very hard without him. I'd have to push through. I'd have to be resilient by trusting God to be my provider and my comforter.

Now, that's me today. That's me, in this modern day of opportunity, admitting that I would still struggle to go on without my husband (not that I couldn't, but that it would be hard). Ruth pushed through with the death of her husband and chose to leave her own people behind to follow Naomi and Naomi's God.

On a side note, imagine how important Naomi's relationship with God had to have been to influence Ruth to want to follow Him, as well.

Ask yourself, "What's not resilient about a woman who leaves everything she knows behind to start a new life? What's not resilient about a woman who suffers the loss of her husband and later accepts the responsibility as provider of her mother-in-law?"

Anyone who has lost anyone can tell you that dealing with loss is a difficult situation. It can take indescribable levels of resilience to cope with the loss. Pushing forward is hard. Persevering is hard. If it wasn't, it wouldn't be described as taking action in the face of difficulty with little likelihood of success.

Ruth not only showed us that it's possible to push forward and persevere, but that it's also possible to comfort someone else during your need for comfort. Ruth was tough. Ruth was strong. Ruth was resilient.

HARD WORK

We're not told whether Ruth worked in the past. Women undoubtedly had household duties that they performed, but unlike blatant descriptions of some women's occupations in the Bible, we don't have that information for Ruth. What we do know is that she worked when she went with Naomi, and she worked hard.

Ruth 2:7 (NLT)

She asked me this morning if she could gather grain behind the harvesters. She has been hard at work ever since, except for a few minutes' rest in the shelter.

It's hard to say a person is resilient without seeing them work. To be resilient requires a person to act. In fact, it means they bounce back from tragedy or hardship, so to do nothing wouldn't seem like a form of resilience. One can hardly be considered resilient if they have done nothing to bounce back after the tragedy.

Think about it. Here's Ruth, now a widow, vowing to take care of her mother-in-law in a foreign land. In addition, she now has to work (maybe for the first time or first time in years). There's no time to lie around and sulk at this point. The only option for survival is to get up and do something. Ruth didn't sit around and wait for a solution or a new man. She went to work.

Ruth 2:2 (NLT)

One day Ruth the Moabite said to Naomi, "Let me go out into the harvest fields to pick up the stalks of grain left behind by anyone who is kind enough to let me do it." Naomi replied, "All right, my daughter, go ahead."

Ruth went to work and it paid off, both literally and figuratively.

In our own lives, what if we've experienced some hardships? What if we've dealt with loss? What if the plan has fallen through? Do we sit and sulk? Ruth would probably say no. Ruth would probably say get up and start changing the narrative, like she did!

A lot of people are waiting for something to happen. They're waiting for the next opportunity, they're waiting for the next movement of God, and they're waiting for it to just happen. But what if God is waiting on them? What if He's waiting on their next move? What if He's waiting on them to trust Him and embark on something new? What about you? What if He's waiting for you to bounce back or at least try? What do you think might have happened if Ruth and Naomi kept waiting? Nothing, probably.

God blesses the wait, but He also blesses godly efforts. The truth is, God can't bless an effort you don't make. Think about it—could God have blessed Ruth with an opportunity like she had with Boaz if she never left the house? If Ruth hadn't been willing to follow Naomi's God (the One and Only God) and start a new life, she might have stayed in Moab. She may have continued to be a part of a nation that was not known for worshiping the One True God. How different would her story have been without pushing forward?

On the flip side, say everything happened as we've read thus far, but Ruth was a lazy worker. The reason Ruth stood out wasn't just because she was new; it was because she was hardworking and loyal. We have to understand: If you can be resilient, you can be hardworking, because resilience is hard work. Look at Ruth. So far, everything

> God can't bless an effort you don't make.

we have read about Ruth's life has been an obstacle. She's not had it easy. Yet, she's still pushing. She's still working hard.

POSITIVE

Now, I'm not saying because you're resilient you're always positive. It's hard to be. When life is hitting you in the face, you're happy to just get back up. You're not trying to be positive; you're just trying to keep standing. Ruth was able to do both.

Perhaps Ruth is resilient because she's positive. I'm not sure, but I want us to look at some of the language Ruth uses. Mind you, this is a woman whose husband has died and who has left a lifestyle she's always known.

Ruth 1:16–17 (NLT)

But Ruth replied, "Don't ask me to leave you and turn back. Wherever you go, I will go; wherever you live, I will live. Your people will be my people, and your God will be my God. Wherever you die, I will die, and there I will be buried. May the Lord punish me severely if I allow anything but death to separate us!"

Ruth 2:2, 10, 13 (NLT)

One day Ruth the Moabite said to Naomi, "Let me go out into the harvest fields to pick up the stalks of grain left behind by anyone who is kind enough to let me do it."

Ruth fell at his feet and thanked him warmly. "What have I done to deserve such kindness?" she asked. "I am only a foreigner."

"I hope I continue to please you, sir," she replied. "You have comforted me by speaking so kindly to me, even though I am not one of your workers."

I know what you're saying, because I'd say it, too. "What do these verses have to do with anything? I thought we were talking about being positive." Well, when I read them, this is what stuck out to me. She's not complaining! She probably doesn't feel like leaving. Maybe she doesn't feel like working. She may be lonely and still grieving the loss of her husband. But she's not complaining, and not complaining makes it more likely to be positive. Don't you find it hard to be negative and resilient at the same time?

It would have been easy for Ruth to complain. Naomi certainly didn't hold it in!

Ruth 1:20-21 (NLT)

"Don't call me Naomi," she responded. "Instead, call me Mara, for the Almighty has made life very bitter for me. I went away full, but the Lord has brought me home empty. Why call me Naomi when the Lord has caused me to suffer and the Almighty has sent such tragedy upon me?"

I'm sure we all know how much easier it is to complain with company, but we don't have any record of Ruth joining in on the pity party. We just see her loyalty, hard work, and obedience.

When faced with difficulty, is that what people can say about us? Could they say we stay positive as we bounce back, or are we just complainers as we push through?

While I understand we can't be positive all the time

(trust me, I'm far from it), we can certainly not be complainers. It's just as easy to praise as it is to complain. I believe that if Ruth had chosen to complain about her misfortune, she would have had a hard time moving forward.

Many of us have convinced ourselves that we've really got it bad. We didn't make the team, we didn't get the job, "it" never works out in our favor, and so on. But what if we at least start to change the way we speak? Could that help? What if we stopped speaking in such negative absolutes?

Do we honestly think we honor God with such verbiage? Do we think that a loving Father wants to hear his daughter speak so negatively? God used words to create life. Shouldn't we do the same?

RUBBER-BAND WOMEN

Why are rubber bands special? They're special because their purpose is to stretch. Their purpose is to expand and go through tension in order to hold something together. Once their job is completed, they bounce back into place. It's hard work, and I'm sure it doesn't feel very good, but because it's resilient, it's used to keep things together.

You're not much different than a rubber band. You go through things that are hard and don't feel good, but because God made you, He can use you to keep things together.

Ruth's resilience didn't just help her survive; it helped keep Naomi afloat, too. Ruth became a provider for both herself and her mother-in-law. Her purpose expanded to something bigger than just herself.

So, who could we help when we keep on pushing? Is there anyone you know that needs to be encouraged to persevere? Remember, as a daughter we are equipped by our Father God, but it's not about Him equipping us for our own use; it's about Him using us to be a blessing to someone or something else.

Where should we be working harder instead of simply waiting longer? After all, work is to be done as unto the Lord (Colossians 3:23).

Lastly, do you need to change your words? Positive words might cause positive outcomes.

Proverbs 15:4 (NLT)
Gentle words are a tree of life; a deceitful tongue crushes the spirit.

Proverbs 16:24 (NLT)
Kind words are like honey—sweet to the soul and healthy for the body.

Proverbs 18:4 (NLT)
Wise words are like deep waters; wisdom flows from the wise like a bubbling brook.

Proverbs 18:20 (NLT)
Wise words satisfy like a good meal; the right words bring satisfaction.

Resilience doesn't come from easy situations.

Do you know the difference between a rubber band and paper clip? Rubber bands can hold different things together. Paper clips were created with the purpose of holding paper together. As you grow and understand resilience, do you want your purpose to expand or stay minimal? Would you rather be a resilient rubber band or a one-purpose paper clip?

Press on, work hard, stop complaining, and see what happens.

RESILIENT RUTH

You had lost it all
How did you not fall?
How were you resilient?
What made you so different?

What made you persevere?
Weren't you afraid? Had you no fear?
Your husband was dead
Did it not lead you to a future to dread?

But you faced it
No, you didn't quit
You believed in Naomi's God
You didn't believe only One was odd

You left the land you knew
To follow what you believed to be true
What was familiar you left behind
It was worth it for what you'd find

An easy life you couldn't afford
You couldn't get bored
You went out and worked hard
You gave easy no regard

You showed great resilience
Through your obedience
And the Lord provided you a spouse
And now your name is a part of His house

D.A.U.G.H.T.E.R.S.

Yes, Boaz came
He gave you his name
There is a descendant of yours you can claim
You are in the lineage of the Name Above All Names

NEVER FORGET

Perseverance is hard, but possible. Resilience doesn't come from easy situations.

Think on It

1. When you face an obstacle, what's the first thing you do? How do you speak about it?
2. Do you believe that hard work requires some resilience? How many times have you had to overcome a situation by working hard?
3. Do you need to change the way you speak? If you were to count the negative words or thoughts you had in one day, would they outweigh the positive?
4. What's been the hardest thing for you to overcome? How did you do it?
5. How can your resilience inspire others?

Scripture Application

Blessed is the one who perseveres under trial because, having stood the test, that person will receive the crown of life that the Lord has promised to those who love him.

—James 1:12 (NIV)

Chapter 9

Successful

If you think you are the entire picture, you will never see the big picture.

—John C. Maxwell

Success can be a tricky word. Success depends on how you define it based on what's important to you. To me, success isn't about things. Success is about having a positive, lasting impact. It's leaving a legacy behind that goes on even after you have gone on. In addition, John Wooden's description was "Success is peace of mind, which is a direct result of self-satisfaction in knowing you made the effort to become the best of which you are capable." Success is peace from knowing that you did your best to be your best. For me, the only way to achieve that type of success is to have a relationship with God, our Heavenly Father.

I am only as successful as my relationship with God is. The two intertwine in my life. I can't have one without the other. It's pretty great. My relationship with God is a real, intentional, successful relationship. Therefore, everything follows that path. If there is no relationship with God, there is no success for me.

So, as you read this chapter, ask yourself, "How does the world define success? How do I define success, and how does God define success?" What He says goes, so if your definition doesn't match His, guess who has gotten it wrong? That's right. You. But since you know it, you can now change it. #GoodNews

All right, so let's talk about Priscilla. She's in the New Testament. Her husband was named Aquila, and they were tentmakers. Paul, who wrote a lot of the New Testament, speaks very highly of them. In case you don't know this, Paul didn't sugarcoat anything, so he must've really been influenced by these people in a good way.

We know it wasn't easy for women back then and that women weren't really meant to have a voice, and certainly a ministry that condoned such was doomed. Yet, you have Paul, the pioneer, calling Priscilla his coworker in the ministry of Christ Jesus.

There is the possibility that success in this century would have been being allowed to speak amongst men. Today, we talk about a glass ceiling for women. Imagine how Priscilla may have felt. Priscilla not only broke through it, she apparently shattered it. A coworker in the ministry of Christ is a pretty awesome way to be described, wouldn't you say?

So, what made her successful? What made her awesome? There's a lot of subtle signs that if we read too fast, we'd miss. So, let's slow down and read some of the verses that reference Priscilla, and then jump into the wonderful traits she had that made her successful by this book's definition.

Acts 18:1–3 (NLT)

Then Paul left Athens and went to Corinth. There he became acquainted with a Jew named Aquila, born in Pontus, who had recently arrived from Italy with his wife, Priscilla. They had left Italy when Claudius Caesar deported all Jews from

Rome. Paul lived and worked with them, for they were tentmakers just as he was.

Acts 18:18 (NLT)

Paul stayed in Corinth for some time after that, then said good-bye to the brothers and sisters and went to nearby Cenchrea. There he shaved his head according to Jewish custom, marking the end of a vow. Then he set sail for Syria, taking Priscilla and Aquila with him.

Acts 18:26 (NLT)

When Priscilla and Aquila heard him preaching boldly in the synagogue, they took him aside and explained the way of God even more accurately.

Romans 16:3–5 (NLT)

Give my greetings to Priscilla and Aquila, my coworkers in the ministry of Christ Jesus. In fact, they once risked their lives for me. I am thankful to them, and so are all the Gentile churches. Also give my greetings to the church that meets in their home.

HONORABLE MENTION

Look through history and you don't see a lot of women names. It's not that we didn't exist; it's just that we weren't really acknowledged. So, it says a lot about Priscilla to be mentioned in company with her husband, Aquila.

You know how we ask who someone's family is? What we mean is who their mother is and father, aunt, or uncle. Who is someone that we know that we can associate that person with? Well, back then a person would only ask who the father is. Lineages were traced through fathers. That's why the genealogy of Jesus is so amazing—it has women in it!

> If you receive your recognition, always be sure to give God His.

What I'm getting at is the fact that Paul didn't necessarily *have* to mention Priscilla in his letters. He could've merely mentioned Aquila, and that would have been fine. It's unique that he would willingly include Priscilla in his letters.

Priscilla got an honorable mention in several letters, so it wasn't like this was a one-time thing. This is how we know Paul was intentional in including Priscilla, a woman.

It's nice to be recognized, isn't it? I don't think it's petty. It's okay to want a little recognition. But this is my advice: Make no mistake in believing that you accomplished anything without God allowing you to. If you receive your recognition, always be sure to give God His.

TEAM PLAYER

A lot of successful people are team players. The very best athletes succeed because of their team, whether they realize it or not. I believe Priscilla was a team player, because in the letters from Paul he includes Priscilla with her husband, Aquila, in his work. To me, it sounds like she joined him in his work, as a good teammate would.

Acts 18:3 said that Paul joined "them," not just Aquila. Even Acts 18:26 says "they" took Apollos (a fellow believer) aside, not just Aquila. Paul says, "*They* have been coworkers," "*They* risked their lives for me," and "I'm not the only one thankful for *them*," not just Aquila in Romans 16:3–5. Clearly, there was a team, and Priscilla was a part of it.

Could anyone say you're a team player? Being a part of a team is similar to being a leader. You come into the team understanding that there is a central goal and you aren't it. You can choose to be a part of achieving that goal, but the overall goal far outweighs the individual. So, ask again, could anyone say that you are a team player?

One thing that doesn't work on a team is an ego. The team that caters to the ego of one person doesn't work very well. It can't. They have to put all their energy into making that one person happy.

> *To win in sports, members of the team must always keep the big picture in front of them. They must remember that the goal is more important than their role—or any individual glory they may desire.*
> —John Maxwell

Have you ever seen a team that doesn't seem as talented as others, but wins? What's their secret? They have singleness of purpose. The purpose is to reach their goal, which is usually to win a championship. The teams with the smallest egos work the best together. Why? Because everyone knows their role and wants to perform in it to win. In this case, winning equals success.

What does being a team player look like in your day? Well, it could look like a few things:

- Do you encourage others? That's our role as Christians, to encourage people.
- Do you make the sacrifice? Do you give up your time—or better yet, your way—for what's best for the team?
- If you're working on a staff project or working on a class project, are you willing to hear everyone else's input and be respectful?
- Are you willing to pick up the slack?
- Are you meeting a need?

This list could go on and on, but I think you get the point. What are you willing to do for the greater good of bringing God glory?

Priscilla and Aquila risked their lives. They let others gather in their home. They let Paul live and work with them. They gave up comfort in order to see the Gospel of Jesus Christ preached. They shared what was theirs to support Paul. And because of it, we have their names in the Bible! We have their service as an example.

God uses people. Could God use you to do as Priscilla and Aquila did? My grandmother reminds me of them. She held a weekly Bible study with food so that her family and friends would hear the gospel outside of regular church attendance. When she passed, my Aunt Dorothy hosted people in her home, and my cousin taught. My Aunt Charlotte would help prepare the food or purchase it. None of this was for personal recognition, but it was for the team. It was for the gospel to be heard. Dare I say, it was to set the example of the gospel of hospitality, as well—which leads to the next thing.

KINDNESS

Priscilla was kind. The Bible says Priscilla and Aquila heard a man preaching boldly in the synagogue, and later took him aside and explained the way of God more accurately in Acts 18:26. They didn't embarrass him by doing it publicly. They cared for him, so they encouraged him to understand God by pulling him aside and spending time with him. They were kind to him. They were kind enough to show respect.

How much differently do you think that man would have felt if publicly Priscilla and Aquila told him that he didn't know enough? He was excited about Jesus, but he only knew so much (Acts 18:24–25). Don't you think he walked away encouraged by the gentle approach of his fellow believers—by the kindness that they showed? They did what we often don't, what we often publicly see people not do: They didn't try to make a big scene and make people feel bad.

Daughter, that's not the way. Has it ever happened to you? Someone really wanted to hurt you or embarrass you, so they did it in front of other people? It feels bad. It makes you not want to try anymore.

Now, think about a time someone addressed you privately. My guess is it was maybe a little hit to your pride, a blow to your ego, but you didn't feel ashamed. You probably felt respected and respected them more for their approach. It maybe even encouraged you to check your own approach toward people, because you received such kindness.

Since we discussed honorable mentions, I'd like to give the word/action "hospitality" an "honorable mention." Hospitality is always respectful and it for sure is kind.

1 Peter 4:9–10 (NIV)

Offer hospitality to one another without grumbling. Each of you should use whatever gift you have received to serve others, as faithful stewards of God's grace in its various forms.

Hospitality makes people feel seen. It makes them feel like they matter.

Remember what I mentioned about my grandmother and her sisters? They weren't hospitable to just family; they also affected a community. Pick either side of my family, and both grandmothers are known for being hospitable.

Hey, I'm a Southerner. We associate hospitality with food a lot, and one thing these ladies did was express hospitality by cooking and inviting people into their homes. They've created a chain reaction, as well. The children all do the same. Why? Because we were so encouraged by their example that we wanted to set the same type of examples. We know what kindness does, so we want to spread it.

We read that Priscilla and Aquila had people in their homes. Paul was one of these people, and he himself said he's not the only one that's thankful for them (Romans 16:5). He even sends his greetings to the church that meets in their home.

Romans 16:5 (NLT)

Also give my greetings to the church that meets in their home.

1 Corinthians 16:19 (NLT)

The churches here in the province of Asia send

greetings in the Lord, as do Aquila and Priscilla and all the others who gather in their home for church meetings.

If hospitality wasn't important, would Paul mention these people for theirs?

Do you ever visit people? When you do, what stands out? For me, what I notice is whether or not they make me feel welcomed. If they do that, I feel even more encouraged to do the same for them one day. I always want to be kind, because I know it softens hearts and situations.

> You can spell care without kindness, but you can't show it without it.

People weren't gathering in Priscilla and Aquila's house without *being* welcomed, and they probably weren't staying without *feeling* welcome. Through that ministry of kindness, I believe they were able to encourage a lot of people toward a relationship with God. Leading people to Jesus by the power of God at work in you is definitely considered a success.

Kindness is a fruit of the Spirit (Galatians 5:22). When the Spirit is working in you, kindness is the result. You can spell "care" without "kindness," but you can't show it without it.

YOUR SUCCESSFUL SELF

You don't have to become exceptional to be successful; you already are. You don't have to be better than anyone else; you just need to be your best self.

Look at Priscilla's story. We don't see any verse that says she was the richest or wisest. We don't see anything that shows she was "exceptional" by the world's definition. But we do gather that she was a team player, and that she was kind and hospitable.

Friend, these aren't impossible characteristics. You can perform any of these acts right now. Even in your own broken state, you can be kind. Even when you need comfort, you can be encouraging. You need support? That doesn't mean you can't be supportive.

You're so special that God would never duplicate you. You are truly one-of-a-kind.

What I'm saying is that you don't have to be perfect to be successful. You don't have to be perfect to be kind. You don't have to be rich to be hospitable. You don't have to be anything but willing to allow God to use you.

You're a success if you choose to be. Don't underestimate yourself, and don't overcomplicate what success is. Success is doing God's will. Success is being your best. Successful accomplishments can be many things:

- Obeying God
- Praying daily
- Finishing a Bible plan
- Serving others
- Finishing a book
- Writing a book
- Treating people with kindness
- Working hard
- Encouraging others
- Being a mentor

The list goes on and on. The thing you have to figure out is how God describes success to you. The next thing is doing it His way. All in all, success is what God tells you it is. Your success is doing His will for you.

You may not own your own business, but you may encourage someone to start one. You may not be the all-star, but you can be a team player. You may not feel like you have anything to give, but kindness is free. Never believe you can't be successful because you are *just* another somebody. You are the only you. You're so special that God would never duplicate you. You are truly one-of-a-kind, which means your impact is, as well.

I believe one of your biggest successes would be seeing yourself as one.

I believe one of your biggest successes would be seeing yourself as one. If you want to truly see yourself, find out what God says about you. He considers you a marvelous work (Psalm 139:14). What's not successful about being God's?

SUCCESS

What if success isn't about the money?
Nor the fame?
Nor the esteem?
What if it's about a different dream?

Success isn't about a gender role
It's about genuinely caring for a soul
Priscilla was a colaborer for Christ
She knew He had paid the price

Success is in His name
In His name there is no shame
It's about being His hands and feet
Knowing the need and choosing to meet

Success may be bold
But it's never meant to be a selfish goal
It's doing what's best for most
And then choosing not to boast

It's about seeing progress
In the middle of the process
It's about support
About being a good sport

If you think success is all about you
Then you've missed the point that's true
It's not about you or me
It's about Jesus who set us free

He was the greatest success of all
He died even for those who would fall
Just think about the cost
That He paid upon the cross

So the next time you acclaim
That success is about being a big name
Remember this simple truth
Success isn't selfish, and Jesus is proof

NEVER FORGET

God measures success differently from the world.

Think on It

1. How do you measure success?
2. How does the world measure success?
3. Who do you consider successful, and why?
4. Why is it important to be kind, a team player, and to build good rapport with people to be successful?
5. How do you think God measures success?

Scripture Application

Therefore, whenever we have the opportunity, we should do good to everyone—especially to those in the family of faith.
—Galatians 6:10 (NLT)

Chapter 10

Once a Daughter, Always a Daughter

See how very much our Father loves us, for he calls
us his children, and that is what we are! But the
people who belong to this world don't recognize that
we are God's children because they don't know him.
—1 John 3:1 (NLT)

My hope is that we all read this book and feel encouraged. I hope that we feel encouraged to make a difference in our lives and in the lives of others. I hope that if you don't know God, you're encouraged to know God, your Heavenly Father, and experience all that He has in store for you.

If you do know God, I hope that you are encouraged to pursue a real relationship with Him—a relationship that is intentional, and purposeful, and understanding of the commitment He has made to you as a Father and Friend, as a Savior and Sacrifice. I hope that you want to spend time with Him and not just learn about Him, but have a truly intimate, authentic relationship with Him.

God loves you. He loves you enough to die for you. Do you love Him? If so, what are you willing to do for Him because you love Him so much? As people who have benefited from the love of God, I hope we do at least three things with it:

1. Love God like crazy
2. Love people like crazy
3. Create a positive impact

LOVE GOD LIKE CRAZY

When I say "crazy," I mean having a devotion that makes no worldly sense, but spiritually makes complete sense. This takes more than just reading our Bibles or books about loving God; this takes intentional work. It takes time and investment. It takes going past what you feel, because you focus on what the relationship needs.

Love sacrifices feelings in order to satisfy fellowship.

For example, I don't always *feel* like loving my husband. I know it sounds mean, but it's true. Love is sacrificial. So, I don't always feel like sacrificing. I don't always feel like putting his needs before mine, but love sacrifices feelings in order to satisfy fellowship.

You won't always feel like praying or reading your Bible. You won't always feel like giving when the Holy Spirit inclines you to do so. But you do it because love obeys God. You do it because obedience glorifies God. You do it because you love God like crazy!

That means being willing to go where you don't want to, to say what you don't want to, to do what you don't feel like doing, because it brings God glory. Because we don't let feelings block faith.

When we love God like crazy, we're willing to sacrifice like crazy, and we're willing to obey like crazy. We're willing to do what doesn't feel good, what doesn't seem normal, and what isn't expected by the world's definition, because we're focused on God.

Loving God like crazy makes you different, and being different is just another word for being unique.

> Being different is just another word for being unique.

LOVE
PEOPLE LIKE CRAZY

People are crazy, so it's hard to love them like crazy. I get that, but you were crazy when God still chose to love you, so don't trip!

Here's the truth: God will never ask you to love or forgive someone any more than He's done for you. In fact, no one can offend you as much as you offended God with your sin. It's hard, but it's true. So, take the forgiveness, take the grace, take the mercy you've received, and give it to others.

Luke 23:33–34 (NLT)

When they came to a place called The Skull, they nailed him to the cross. And the criminals were also crucified—one on his right and one on his left. Jesus said, "Father, forgive them, for they don't know what they are doing."

As Jesus was dying, He prayed for people's forgiveness. Surely, we can do that as we're living. The best way to begin doing this is to see people as God sees us all. We are all in need of a Savior, and a lot of times how we love is what leads people to or from Jesus.

I vote that we set the example of love by following Jesus's example: loving, serving, giving, and showing kindness. Jesus loved. He served, He gave, He forgave, He

> As Jesus was dying, He prayed for people's forgiveness. Surely, we can do that as we're living.

was kind, and He was compassionate. Jesus *did* love. He didn't just say He loved people. He didn't just write about love. He did love and gave us an example to follow.

Let's love people the way Jesus loves us. Let's love people to Jesus.

Ephesians 5:1–2 (NLT)

Imitate God, therefore, in everything you do, because you are his dear children. Live a life filled with love, following the example of Christ. He loved us and offered himself as a sacrifice for us, a pleasing aroma to God.

CREATE A POSITIVE IMPACT

I believe we should love God and love people. I believe that doing those things automatically creates a positive impact. We love God and love His creation, and as we do that, we begin to hurt when we see His creation do things that hurt themselves and others.

It hurts me to see so many discouraged young ladies and women. It hurts me to hear about sex trafficking. It hurts me to hear about people discouraging others. It hurts me to know that there are people who don't know Jesus and don't care.

So, what hurts you? Do you have a heart for those who have been abused? Do you have a passion to fight racism? Does it hurt you to know the statistics of homelessness in our country? What about the persecution of people throughout the world?

Identify what hurts you and choose to bring awareness

to it. When we are in alignment with God, He will use us. Whatever the cause is that God has truly put on your heart, ask Him what He wants you to do about it.

Seeing women discouraged, lost, or questioning their value hurts me. It truly hurts me. God put this book on my heart to write in response to that hurt. Currently, I'm in the process of putting together a conference in my hometown to encourage young women to live as daughters, which was the original idea before this book.

How can you get started? Maybe it's by just writing down what you see. Maybe it's researching the statistics and history of the dilemma. Could there be a website or organization you can raise funds for? It starts by asking yourself, "Where can I start?" Then take the next step: Find an organization that supports your calls, and find the needs they have that you can meet.

If it doesn't exist, spend time in prayer asking God if you should create it. We love God and love His people; we want what's best for them. We're willing to sacrifice time, energy, and money to positively impact them. So, because you love God and His people, what's your cause, and what's your sacrifice for it? God's cause was the salvation of people. His sacrifice was Himself. Surely, we can invest in the people He chose to sacrifice Himself for.

> Find out what breaks your heart and do something about it.

WALK IN PURPOSE ON PURPOSE

I love you. I don't know you, and I don't have to know you to love you. And as great as it is for you—sense the sarcasm—I have even better news. God loves you. He does know everything about you, and He still loves you.

This story is your story. We're different. Daughters are different. You are different. The beauty in being a daughter is that you are always one.

God is a Good Father. Good fathers don't pick and choose when to love their daughters; they always do. Even when we disobey, even when we disengage, even when we don't like Him or others as we should, He loves us.

In His love for us, He's made us daughters. He's made us dynamic, authentic, unique, gracious, hopeful, triumphant, empowered, resilient, successful, and then some—in Him.

God could have not made you, but He loves you enough to create you. Do you love Him enough to let Him use you to share His love with others? Daughters, there are sons that need His love. There are mothers and fathers that need His love. There are people who don't know Him. What are we going to do about it? What are you going to do about it?

Walk in purpose today and every day. Love God, your Father. Love others, people your Father created. Live as a daughter, as an heiress, and as a game changer. Just like the women that we read about in this book, you can make a difference. You never know who's watching, and you never know who will be affected by you. Therefore, use your influence to glorify and honor God.

God loved you enough to create you, and He created you with a purpose. Are you going to love Him enough to live it out?

Mark 12:29–31 (NLT)
Jesus replied, "The most important commandment

is this: 'Listen, O Israel! The Lord our God is the one and only Lord. And you must love the LORD your God with all your heart, all your soul, all your mind, and all your strength.' The second is equally important: 'Love your neighbor as yourself.' No other commandment is greater than these."

YOU MATTER

You matter
I know it's easy to forget that with all of the banter
You were created with a purpose on purpose
Don't doubt this

There is only one you
Your purpose is true
God didn't make two
So do what He created you to do

That person who made you question and made you
wonder
He or she that made you ponder
Whether you had an impact
Was wrong, in fact

Jesus loved you so much that He died
He laid aside all pride
To see you succeed
He chose to bleed

So don't waste a second
Wondering if what they said is true
Who cares what they say
Jesus knows you

NEVER FORGET

God loves His children.

Think on It

1. Do you love God?
2. Do you love His people?
3. What causes tug at your heart?
4. How can you begin a plan of action to support that cause?
5. What's one way you can express love to someone? Can you do this daily, or at least weekly?
6. What does being a daughter truly mean to you?

Scripture Application

And since we are his children, we are his heirs. In fact, together with Christ we are heirs of God's glory. But if we are to share his glory, we must also share his suffering.
　　　　　　　　　　　　　　　—Romans 8:17 (NLT)

Acknowledgments

Dear Lord, you used David to say it best: "Who am I [. . .] and what is my family, that you have brought me this far" (2 Samuel 7:18, NLT)? Who am I that You would use my mind and my hands to write such beautiful messages from You? Thank You for every word, every idea, every effort, every encouragement, and every truth from You.

To my mommy—there aren't a lot of words that top a mother's approval and love. I've received your love and encouragement throughout this project. The moment you said, "This is excellent," is cemented in my mind and heart.

Thank you, Caitlin and Libby. You read and made notes for hours. While you saw this book, God saw your heart to help. Words can't express how much I appreciate your time and input.

Christy, because I know you and your humility, I won't say what you did. Just know it was right on time, as Brandon and I prayed for guidance and signs from God.

The Morgan family, thank you for all your prayers.

Brandon, my love, thank you for your support. Thank you for this amazing cover. Thank you for being you. God knew what I needed, and He knew what I wanted, and yet He went above and beyond, and blessed me with you.

To my family—your support is indescribable. I want to make you all proud! You are my family and my friends. Mom, Dad, GG, Lene, Maya, and Brandon, thank you for being a part of the reading team in the final push! #RiceCovenant #TuckerFamily

BookLogix, thank you for your time and input. You sought to make this project good, and we did that.

Lord, thank You for the readers' time. I pray that they were and are able to know Your love for them during this time. Grant them Your wisdom and guidance, and please allow them to know Your love for them as Your daughters. Bless and keep them, and make Your face shine upon them (Numbers 6:24–25). In Jesus's name, amen.

About the Author

Chanel Moore is a teacher at Covenant Christian Academy; like many in her family, she has found a love for education. She is married to her husband, Brandon, and they are members of Victory Church in Norcross, Georgia.

When Brandon and Chanel are not working on books, they are spending time together doing their podcast, MooreTime, and spending time with family and friends.

In addition, she and Brandon, along with Chanel's brother, have their own online apparel store, Chosen Designs Online. Chanel also contributes to the devotional app Devotable.

In the near future, D.A.U.G.H.T.E.R.S. the conference will begin. For more details on it, you can visit Chanel's website at www.achanelmoore.com.

Other Books
by Chanel Moore

Know Now What You'll Wish You Had Known Back Then

Study This Book Devotional